Thomas Hardy's

Jude the Obscure

Text by
Cynthia C. Jones
(M.A., New York University)
Department of English
Evander Childs High School
Bronx, New York
and
Laurie Kalmanson
(M.A., University of Chicago)

Illustrations by
Bob Rodefeld

Research & Education Association

What **MAXnotes**® *Will Do for You*

This book is intended to help you absorb the essential contents and features of Thomas Hardy's *Jude the Obscure* and to help you gain a thorough understanding of the work. The book has been designed to do this more quickly and effectively than any other study guide.

For best results, this **MAXnotes** book should be used as a companion to the actual work, not instead of it. The interaction between the two will greatly benefit you.

To help you in your studies, this book presents the most up-to-date interpretations of every section of the actual work, followed by questions and fully explained answers that will enable you to analyze the material critically. The questions also will help you to test your understanding of the work and will prepare you for discussions and exams.

Meaningful illustrations are included to further enhance your understanding and enjoyment of the literary work. The illustrations are designed to place you into the mood and spirit of the work's settings.

The **MAXnotes** also include summaries, character lists, explanations of plot, and section-by-section analyses. A biography of the author and discussion of the work's historical context will help you put this literary piece into the proper perspective of what is taking place.

The use of this study guide will save you the hours of preparation time that would ordinarily be required to arrive at a complete grasp of this work of literature. You will be well prepared for classroom discussions, homework, and exams. The guidelines that are included for writing papers and reports on various topics will prepare you for any added work which may be assigned.

The **MAXnotes** will take your grades "to the max."

Dr. Max Fogiel
Program Director

Contents

**Each Section includes List of Characters,
Summary, Analysis, Study Questions and
Answers, and Suggested Essay Topics.**

SECTION ONE

Introduction

The Life and Works of Thomas Hardy

Jude the Obscure is the last novel written by Thomas Hardy, an author whose work reflects both his personal life and the intellectual trends of nineteenth-century England. Thomas Hardy was born June 2, 1840 in Higher Bockhampton, Dorset, England. He was the eldest of four children. His father started a successful building and contracting business with an initial stake of only fourteen pounds. His mother was Jemima Hand, who worked as a maidservant and received pauper relief, a sort of welfare program. Thomas Hardy had a complicated attitude toward his family origins. He had a particular interest, common to many born into humble circumstances, in being accepted by upper-class society. Hardy was also convinced that his ancestors had formerly been successful and important but had recently come down in the world.

The young Thomas was a delicate child who learned to read at about three years of age. He played with the local peasant children as a young boy, but his parents forbade him to use their rural dialect. His mother arranged for his education and tutoring, first at the village school and later at Dorchester Day School.

His childhood was reasonably happy. Long hours were spent roaming the countryside on his own. His parents encouraged his interests in music and reading. As an adolescent, he became acquainted with the poet William Barnes, who lived in Dorset. Barnes was to have a strong influence on Hardy.

As a teenager, Hardy taught himself Greek and began to write poetry. He wanted to become a member of the clergy, but his formal education was never advanced enough to qualify him for such a profession. Despite his eventual accomplishments, he felt ashamed of his relative lack of schooling his entire life. Religion also played an important role in Hardy's early life. Like most of the rural middle class, the Hardys were Anglicans.

At sixteen, Hardy was apprenticed to a Dorchester architect, John Hicks. In 1862 he left Dorchester for London to work as assistant to the architect Arthur Blomfield. While in London, he developed his intellectual tastes by attending the opera, theatres, and museums, and by reading progressive and skeptical authors such as Charles Darwin, John Stuart Mill, Herbert Spencer, and T. H. Huxley, among others.

He never attended university, but was tutored during his apprenticeship by a Cambridge student named Horace Moule. Moule's early death caused Hardy great sadness. Hardy's lack of a degree always caused him some remorse, though it did not particularly limit his life. He was to meet some of the great intellectual figures of his day, including George Meredith, the novelist who would give him advice on publication.

In 1867 Hardy returned to Higher Bockhampton, and though his initial writing attempts were poems, his prolific writing career really began with *The Poor Man and the Lady*, now lost. *The Poor Man and the Lady* is a story contrasting London and the countryside, which Hardy completed in 1868 at age twenty-eight while working for John Hicks. The influential critic and author George Meredith advised Hardy not to publish the book but encouraged him to write another. *The Poor Man and the Lady* was rejected by publishers as being too satiric in tone. His second attempt at a novel, *Desperate Remedies*, was published in 1871 by William Tinsley to mixed reviews.

Hardy soon decided to concentrate in his novels on what he knew and loved best, the social life of rural southern England. After two moderately successful novels, *Under the Greenwood Tree* (1872) and *A Pair of Blue Eyes* (1873), were published anonymously, Hardy scored a significant success in 1874 with *Far from the Madding Crowd*. After his triumph, he married Emma Lavinia Gifford, whom he had met several years earlier.

Hardy continued writing novels of "Wessex," the historical, Anglo-Saxon name he gave in fiction to his native Dorset, from this time until 1895. *Tess of the D'Urbervilles*, published in 1891, was immediately popular with the reading public. However it also caused controversy. Victorian moralists and ecclesiastics were scandalized by the author's contention that his heroine was, in the words of the novel's subtitle, a morally pure woman. Some readers were outraged by the book's pessimism, by the unrelieved picture of torment and misery Hardy presented. Orthodox believers in God were scandalized by his suggestions that the beneficent warm God of Christianity seemed absent from the world Hardy depicted.

After the bitter denunciation of the sexual double standard in *Tess*, Hardy expanded his satiric attack in his next novel, *Jude the Obscure* (1895), which criticized the institutions of marriage, the Church, and England's class system. Again Hardy was savaged by critics who could not countenance his subversiveness. He was attacked in the press as decadent, indecent, and degenerate. Among those offended was his wife, who took the novel as anti-religious, and thus a blow to the devoutness she believed she shared with her husband. Distressed by such small-mindedness, Hardy, now financially secure, vowed to give up novel-writing and return to the composition of poetry, his first literary love, which he felt would afford him greater artistic and intellectual freedom. From 1898 on Hardy published mainly poetry. He became one of the few English authors to produce a significant body of poetry as well as novels.

Hardy had no children but his marriages were extremely significant factors in his life and can be seen as having a strong effect on his work. He was in love several times and once engaged to a maid named Eliza Nicholls before meeting his first wife. In 1870, he met Emma Gifford on a trip to Cornwall, and married her in 1874. Her family disapproved of the marriage and considered Hardy beneath Emma. Though Hardy loved Emma, the marriage became unhappy, but continued until her death in 1912. Later, Hardy looked back on her with affection.

Throughout his life, Hardy became infatuated with seemingly unattainable women. While Emma was still alive, he carried on an intense correspondence with Mrs. Florence Henniker, a writer who lived in Dublin. She was to have a great influence on Hardy. Meanwhile, Emma had become fanatically religious and nearly insane. After Emma's death he married Florence Dugdale, who had been his secretary and literary aide for several years. The second marriage proved happier. Florence Hardy wrote a biography of her husband, part of which was dictated by Hardy himself.

Hardy and Emma lived at Newton from 1875 until 1878, when they moved to Upper Tooting. While living in Newton, Hardy wrote *The Return of the Native* (1878). In 1885, Hardy and Emma moved to Dorset. There he wrote *The Mayor of Casterbridge* (1886), *The Woodlanders* (1887), *Tess of the D'Urbervilles* (1891), and finally, *Jude the Obscure*, which was published in 1896. This was to be his last novel.

In 1898, Thomas Hardy published *Wessex Poems*. On the whole, his poetry is not nearly so well regarded as his novels, but is still considered to have merit.

After the turn of the century, he worked on *The Dynasts*, an epic-drama in verse of the Napoleonic wars, published in three volumes from 1903 to 1908. In 1910 he was awarded the Order of Merit and in 1912 he finished revising all his novels, rendering them exactly as he wanted them. In November of 1912, Emma Hardy died after a long illness, through which her husband did not give her very much aid.

An aspect of Hardy's childhood which is of more importance in *Jude the Obscure* than in all of his other novels is that of religion. Hardy had abandoned Christianity while in London, but returned to his faith later on. Though *Jude the Obscure* portrays a world in which God appears to be absent, the characters are constantly reacting to religious teaching.

Important themes common to many of the novels include questioning the institution of marriage, the interaction between man and nature, class conflict, and the role of women in nineteenth century society. In addition to Wessex, he assigned fictional names to other real locations. Thus, Marygreen is Fawley, Christminster is Oxford, etc. This simultaneously lends a realism to the work, while giving Hardy license to shape his fictional world. One strong similarity between the real and fictional world, however, is the tension between London and the countryside. On the one hand, modern influences were sought after by the country people and on the other, they were resented and seen as threatening. Hardy frequently writes in dialect, showing the different speech patterns of various classes. Though he was essentially of a middle-class background, he treats his working class characters sympathetically.

Hardy's attitude toward his characters, particularly his female characters, is extraordinarily complex. His most famous female characters include Sue Bridehead of *Jude the Obscure*, Bathsheba Everdene of *Far from the Madding Crowd*, and Tess from *Tess of the D'Urbervilles*. They portray great strength, but are also prone to great weakness. Of these, Sue Bridehead is probably the most complex. *Jude the Obscure* was written while Hardy's first wife, Emma, was still alive. It is not difficult to see a dissatisfaction with marriage evident in the novel, which presumably reflects his marital problems. Sue Bridehead can be seen as a sort of romantic fantasy, someone Hardy wished he had married. The fact that the relationship between Sue and Jude fails reflects not just Hardy's pessimism, but his unwillingness to make an adulterous relationship successful. No actual adultery on his part was ever proved.

Certainly, there are other parallels between Hardy's own life and the portrayal of Jude, though it was far from autobiographical. Hardy himself was apprenticed to an architect, Jude was a stone mason who did church reconstruction, like Hardy's father. Hardy studied Greek on his own, as Jude does. Finally, at age twenty-six, Hardy was in love with his cousin, Tryphena Sparks who, at sixteen was studying to become a teacher. It is difficult not to believe that this was the source for the character of Sue Bridehead, although she is also said to be based on Florence Henniker. It is clear that Hardy preferred to write about the world of his childhood and adolescence rather than the more sophisticated world in which he moved as an adult. In none of his novels, and particularly not in *Jude*, was the Wessex countryside overly sentimentalized. Though he saw its beauty, he also saw its dark side.

Hardy's last two novels, *Tess of the D'Urbervilles* and *Jude the Obscure*, were his most controversial. *Jude the Obscure*, like many novels of the time, was published serially both in England and the

United States. The American version was "cleaned up" so as to be suitable for all ages. References to extramarital relations were deleted, as were the gruesome deaths.

Hardy continued to receive honors and degrees in the first decades of the 1900s, including honorary degrees in literature from Cambridge University in 1913 and Oxford University in 1920. On January 11, 1928, Thomas Hardy died. His biography was published posthumously the same year. His ashes were placed in Poets' Corner of Westminster Abbey. His heart was buried in his first wife's grave at Stinsford next to the grave of his parents.

Historical Background

Thomas Hardy lived at a time of intense and rapid social change in England, and his novels reflect on many of these changes, especially those affecting his native Dorset.

Hardy's career as a novelist roughly paralleled the late Victorian era, named after Britain's Queen Victoria, who reigned from 1837 to 1901. The Victorian period was an era of change and paradox which cannot be easily summarized.

Victorians were known for prudishness about sex. Though there has been debate over the veracity of this generalization, certainly *Jude the Obscure* was written against the backdrop of a somewhat repressive society. Even more than London, rural England was known for its conservative morals. In particular, the Evangelicals, a segment of the Anglican church, advocated self-denial and sobriety. Certainly, however, there were plenty who deviated from this harsh code. Jude's propensity to drink is not atypical. Women at the time were engaged in the struggle for the right to vote, which did not come until 1918. As early as 1792, Mary Wollstonecraft had published *A Vindication of the Rights of Women*, questioning the restrictions society placed on women. In 1869 John Stuart Mill had published "The Subjection of Women" in which he advocated both suffrage and the opportunity for women to pursue careers. However, changes in laws and social customs were slow in coming. The field of novel-writing had, of course, many female practitioners. Still, in order that she be taken seriously, Mary Ann Evans wrote under the name George Eliot. The first college for women in England had opened in 1847, but educational opportunities for women in Hardy's time were still far fewer than those available to men.

England in the 1890s was also considering "The Marriage Question"; that is, whether such unions could be legally dissolved. Hardy's writing on this issue can be seen as being affected by his personal life and the contemporary social debate. An important corollary of this issue was the right of a married woman to hold property. The Married Women's Property Acts, passed between 1870 and 1908, ended the practice of giving all control of any property inherited or purchased by a woman to her husband.

However, several Victorian issues, such as economic growth and dislocation, religious and moral controversy, and the question of women's liberation, remind us of contemporary social problems.

In the first six decades of the nineteenth century, England's gross national product grew by more than four hundred percent. Industrialization, which allowed for increased trade both in England and abroad, was the cause of this vast upsurge in national and in some cases personal wealth. Innovations in communication and travel, particularly railways, facilitated the operations of industry and the flow of money. By the second half of the nineteenth century, England had become a country based on urban industry rather than feudal land-owning.

It is frequently said in economics that a rising tide lifts all boats—that progress and growth benefit every member of society. From personal and historical knowledge, Hardy knew this statement to contain substantial untruth. Victorian society hotly debated the ultimate value of its unprecedented economic expansion. Workers were paid more, many businessmen became rich, and England became the dominant economic power of the world, but some groups of society felt it no longer afforded them a place at all. Agricultural and unskilled rural workers particularly were subject to dislocation and upheaval as farmwork became less profitable than factory work, even though most factory work was degrading and dangerous and entailed living in crowded and unhealthy cities and towns.

The demographic or population statistics tell a staggering story. The 1851 census showed that for the first time more people lived in towns and cities than the countryside, a finding that fascinated the Victorians. Over the 1800s, England's population grew from 8.9 to 32.5 million. The population of London rose sixfold over the same period, while the number of towns with a population over 50,000 went from 7 to 57. A move from the country to a city frequently meant the loss of a home and the loss of generations' worth of social traditions. One commentator, indicating the dangers of such population shifts, wrote it was apparent "that the towns are gaining at the expense of the country, whose surplus population they absorb and destroy."

Another prominent feature of life in Hardy's England was a widespread loss of religious faith. In large part this was sparked by the writings of Charles Darwin, the naturalist whose discovery of evolution put much of the Bible into serious doubt for many people. Many intellectuals abandoned their religious beliefs, including Hardy, to an extent. Denied the emotional consolation of religion, many Victorians felt that ultimate questions of human existence (Who are we? Where are we going?) were unanswerable, leaving them in confusion, feeling what Hardy calls the "ache of modernism."

Darwin's theory of the extinction of species which could not adapt to change was especially important to Hardy. Influenced by Darwin, he saw Nature and the world in unsentimental fashion, as sites of cruelty, struggle, and death. Hardy even felt that classes and groups of people could become extinct if the historical conditions which supported their existence were taken away. He feared that the class his family came from, the rural laborers, might be completely destroyed if its existence was no longer useful to society. Their customs, their way of life, their style of thinking, could be lost forever, shoved aside by a new bourgeois class which made a feudal-based labor system irrelevant. Hardy perceived contemporary events as part of the flow of history and driven by forces beyond individual human control.

Meanwhile, the loss of religious faith sparked general fears about a breakdown in morality. Without a foundation in religion, and without the reference point of a common religious practice, how could morality be enforced or even expected? The redistribution of wealth, power, and population effected by the Industrial Revolution combined with the atmosphere of religious doubt to lead many to conclude that England's moral fabric was being torn asunder. In *Jude the Obscure*, Hardy uses the central characters to set up debates on the issues of religion and morality.

Another Victorian controversy of importance was the issue of how women should be viewed and what roles they should play in society. Many felt that women were outfitted only for work in the home, and were not capable of education or professional achievement. Writers described the world as being made up of two spheres, the home and the public world, and tried to prove that woman's place was only in the home. Victorian women were supposed to be an angel in the house and nothing more. Although this angelic status was primarily a middle-class ideal, it shows the intense Victorian devotion to the idea of female innocence. Many Victorians felt that if a woman lost her honor, or virginity, before marriage, then she was irreparably harmed, and must bear the shame the rest of her life. The plight of the so-called fallen woman was central to Victorian morality. No such prohibition was attached to male sexual behavior.

Jude the Obscure is filled with references to contemporary intellectual figures, and reflects many of the trends in late Victorian English thought. These include the conflict between the religious and the secular and what was known as "The Woman Question." Hardy held progressive views on these issues.

One of the most important developments of Victorian England was the establishment of schools for the rural working class. Hardy attended such a school and, no doubt, Jude's opportunity to have the education that he had was a result of this. Other trends to influence Hardy's youth were chartism, which brought greater rights for the working class, and the railroad, which connected the countryside to London.

The nineteenth century is typically divided between the Romantic Age and the Victorian Age, and while Hardy's work certainly falls chronologically in the Victorian Age, he has much in common with the Romantics. Like Wordsworth, he preferred to write about the common man and nature rather than upper-class society. Unlike Wordsworth, however, he had actually lived in the milieu about which he wrote. Hardy's rural characters were not just sentimentalized, but realistic. Certainly, however, the introduction of such topics by Wordsworth paved the way for making Hardy's work acceptable to the Victorian reader.

While Wordsworth is in the background, the work of another Romantic poet, Percy Shelley, is an integral part of *Jude the Obscure*. Shelley was far more overtly political than Wordsworth, and he speaks to both the relationship between Jude and Sue and to the conflicts they feel with the world around them. Though Shelley attended University, he was a rebel. Poems quoted in *Jude* include "The Revolt of Islam" and "Epipsychidion."

The novel was published at the end of the Victorian Era. Optimism and expansion, hallmarks of Victorianism, were no longer appealing to Hardy and many of his contemporaries. The struggle for Empire which took place throughout the nineteenth century did not, Hardy believed, improve England's social climate. He was considered by many to be a pessimist, though he denied that this was so. Certainly, his novels were not so optimistic as those of earlier Victorian novelists, such as Dickens and Charlotte Bronte.

In Dickens' and Bronte's novels, things had a way of working out. Extraordinary coincidences reunited families, and bad people were punished. Though the novels were critical of society, they also fit in with the notion of progress; the quality of life in general was improving due to the Industrial Age. Hardy, however, rejects this belief in progress, as is evident in the outcome of his novels, particularly that of *Jude*. Good and evil are not so clearly separated and, certainly, good does not prevail. This aspect of Hardy's work looks ahead to modernism.

Jude the Obscure was an extraordinarily controversial work, though Hardy was taken aback by this controversy. The novel was seen as a threat to marriage and social order; he denied that it was a treatise on evil, but merely the story of two individuals. Critics were particularly offended by Sue Bridehead, who questioned both the need for marriage and the general subservience of women. That he did not anticipate a negative reaction is surprising, since several of his previous novels, particularly *Tess of the D'Urbervilles*, met with such a response. It is possible that this adverse reaction to the novel led Hardy to turn to poetry.

Master List of Characters

Jude Fawley—*The title character. He begins life as a poor ward in a quiet village and becomes a stonecutter. He dreams of being an educated man and falls in love with his cousin, Sue Bridehead.*

Richard Phillotson—*Schoolmaster who is Jude's early mentor. He marries Sue Bridehead. He nurtures his own dreams of social and intellectual advancement.*

Blacksmith and Farm Bailiff—*Villagers who help Phillotson move.*

Drusilla Fawley—*Jude's great-aunt; she raises him after his parents die. She is coarse and ignorant.*

Farmer Troutham—*The farmer who catches Jude encouraging birds to eat his grain.*

Villagers—*People to whom the Fawley's familys history is told.*

Carter—*A workman who meets Jude on the road.*

Two Workmen—*Help Jude climb on the roof of a barn to see Christminster.*

Physician Vilbert—*The quack doctor who promises and fails to deliver Greek and Latin texts to Jude.*

Arabella Donn—*The pig-keeper's daughter. An ambitious, coarse, materialistic, deceitful woman. Jude's wife.*

Mr. Donn & Mrs. Donn—*Arabella's parents, pig-keepers. Jude and Arabella live with them after they are married the second time.*

Anny and Sarah—*Young women; Arabella's friends and confidantes.*

Challow—*The pig killer who arrives late, forcing Jude and Arabella to kill a pig.*

Sue Bridehead—*Jude's cousin, true love, and soul-mate. Impulsive, idealistic, intellectual, school-teacher. She marries Phillotson.*

Mrs. Edlin—*Friend of Jude's aunt.*

Vendor—*Marketer of religious icons. He sells pagan statues to Sue.*

Miss Fontover—*Sue's employer and first landlady in Christminster. She breaks Sue's statues.*

Mrs. Hawes—*Sue's second landlady in Christminster. Chaperones Phillotson's tutoring session with Sue.*

John Marygreen—*Villager who asks Jude about Christminster.*

Shepherd and his mother—*Country people who invite Sue and Jude to spend the night in their home.*

Uncle Jim, Uncle Joe—*Stonemasons who drink with Jude and attend his second wedding to Arabella.*

Undergraduates—*Encourage Jude to recite in Latin in a bar.*

Tinker Taylor—*A blasphemous iron worker with whom Jude drinks.*

Mr. Highridge—*A curate, encourages Jude to enter the clergy.*

Neighbor—*Confirms Drusilla's stories about Sue.*

Students at Sue's College—*Busybodies who spread rumors about Sue after she spends the night away from school.*

Miss Traceley—*School official whose duties include roll call.*

Porter—*The school worker who hears splashing in the river.*

Jude's Landlady—*The landlady at Melchester.*

Nurse—*Woman who looks after Jude's great-aunt.*

Mr. Cockman—*Flirts with Arabella.*

The Undergraduate—*Mentioned in conversation; deceased student with whom Sue had a long intellectual relationship.*

The Musician—*Author of a piece of religious music; rejects Jude because the stonecutter is a poor man.*

Gillingham—*Supports Phillotson when Sue leaves.*

Waiting Maid—*Hotel staff member who tells Sue that Jude was there with Arabella.*

Chairman of the School Committee—*Fires Phillotson when he finds out that Sue is gone.*

Itinerants—*People who defend Phillotson at his public hearing after Sue has left.*

Mr. Carlett—*Arabella's second husband.*

Little Father Time—*Jude's son by Arabella. He is being raised by Sue and Jude along with their two children.*

Biles and Willis—*Contractors who hire Jude to help restore a church.*

Old Vicar and Churchwarden—*Church officials at a building where Sue is helping Jude do a restoration job.*

Church-Cleaner, Village Women—*Gossips who make it impossible for Jude and Sue to work at the church.*

Little Girl—*Lets Jude into the house in Shaston.*

Minister—*Marries Phillotson and Sue in Melchester.*

Ada—*Servant who brings tea to Jude and Sue in Shaston schoolhouse.*

Guard—*Attendant on train carrying Little Father Time to Aldbrickham.*

Working Woman and Other Passengers—*Little Father Time's companions on the trip to Aldbrickham.*

Collector—*Directs Little Father Time to Jude's house.*

Soldier and his Bride—*Couple whose wedding Jude and Sue observe at the registry.*

Messenger—*Informs Jude of a job at the church in Aldbrickham.*

Charwomen and Two Ladies—*Gossip about Sue's marital status.*

Auctioneer—*Sells Jude's and Sue's belongings.*

Two Children—*Born to Sue and Jude.*

Surgeon—*Tries to help the two children.*

Woman in the Crowd—*Comments on Jude's fatigued appearance.*

Coach Driver—*A man who savagely mistreats his horse while a crowd watches.*

Jack Stagg—*A man who recognizes Jude during the Remembrance Day celebration at Christminster.*

Policeman—*Reacts to the Coach Driver beating the horse.*

Landladies—*Reject Jude's and Sue's requests for housing.*

Third Landlady's Husband—*Orders his wife not to house Sue and Jude.*

Carpenter and his Wife—*Landlord and landlady of the lodgings Sue and Jude take after the children are dead.*

Summary of the Novel

Jude is an eleven-year-old orphan living with his great-aunt in Marygreen, a provincial town about 20 miles from Christminster, the university modeled after Oxford. Although of working class background, he develops an interest in getting a university education. Richard Phillotson, the former schoolmaster, sends him old Greek and Latin textbooks and Jude begins to study for several years on his own, while working first as a bakery cart driver and then as an apprentice to a stonemason.

However, his studies are interrupted when he meets and marries Arabella, whose earthiness and ambition stand in contrast to his own dreaminess. Arabella convinces him to marry by pretending to be pregnant. After he finds out that she is not pregnant, the marriage goes sour and she goes off to Australia with her family, although the marriage is never legally dissolved.

Jude then moves to Christminster in hopes of entering the university, and finds work as a stonemason. At his aunt's he has seen a picture of his cousin, Sue Bridehead, whom he has never met. He is attracted to her picture, but his aunt warns him not to meet her, as she holds Sue's side of the family in low regard. However, Jude does meet her and is drawn to her intellect and unconventional spirit. Her religious beliefs could be categorized as pagan. She has taught school, but is working in Christminster for a maker of ecclesiastical statuary. She has read Gibbon and Mill, and has an intellect and social sophistication that Jude lacks. For a time, she lived in London with a university student. However, she remains a virgin, not for conventionally moral reasons, but in order to preserve her integrity.

Soon after Jude finds Sue, he also contacts Richard Phillotson, his old schoolmaster. He introduces Sue and Phillotson. Phillotson gives her a job in his school, then he, too, falls in love with her. At about the same time, Jude is told by the university officials that someone of his class would be better off without a degree. Jude, despondent, endeavors to pursue a life in the church. He moves to Melchester to pursue this course of action, and to be near Sue. He continues until the end of the novel to work as a stonemason, finding that his passions are stronger than his spiritual interest. Sue attends a training college for teachers in Melchester, but is expelled after she misses her curfew when she and Jude stay out all night.

Shortly thereafter, fearing that her reputation will be ruined by her expulsion, Sue marries Phillotson, and they both teach at a school in Shaston. However, Jude and Sue continue to correspond and visit. Sue confides that she is not happy in her marriage. They are brought together by the death of Great-Aunt Drusilla. On this occasion, they kiss for the first time. Eventually, Sue agrees to leave Phillotson and live with Jude. Phillotson gives his consent to her departure; when his superiors at the school discover the arrangement, Phillotson is relieved of his position.

Jude and Sue do not get married, despite the fact that Jude asks Sue to do so on several occasions. Their decision not to marry is based in part on the emotional consequences of their loveless marriages and in part in their belief that both are afflicted by a hereditary curse on marriage. Neither Jude's nor Sue's parents had happy marriages, and Great-Aunt Drusilla has told them that they are beset by an ancient curse. Jude is willing to put aside these fears, but Sue's marriage to Phillotson has led her to despise the institution, much as Jude's problems with Arabella Donn had caused him to be fearful.

While Jude and Sue are living in Aldbrickham, Jude learns from Arabella that he has a son who is nicknamed Little Father Time. The boy comes to live with Jude and Sue. The fact that they are not married causes the child they are raising to be ostracized.

Jude loses his job. They move, first to Kennetsbridge where they have two children of their own, and, after Jude becomes ill, back to Christminster. Little Father Time, overwhelmed by the problems of his parents, hangs the other children and himself. Both Jude and Sue are devastated, but Sue, in particular, reacts by renouncing all her liberal ideas and turning, fanatically, to religion. She believes that the tragedy occurred because God intended that she remain married to Phillotson and that Jude remain with Arabella. She believes she has gone against God's will. When she goes back to Phillotson, Jude returns to Arabella, who has for some time been plotting to get him back. While he is drunk, she tricks him into marrying her again. They live in Christminster with Arabella's father. However, Jude has lost the will to live. He falls ill and dies while Arabella is out celebrating. Only Arabella and Widow Edlin attend the funeral.

Estimated Reading Time

The novel is divided into six sections, entitled "At Marygreen", "At Christminster", "At Melchester", "At Shaston", "At Aldbrickham and Elsewhere", and "At Christminster Again". In each section, Jude lives at that location. The number of chapters within each section varies.

Jude the Obscure is a fairly dense novel and will probably take the average reader at least eight hours to finish. By reading the novel in the same way it was structured, a section at a time, rather than chapter by chapter, the author's intentions will become apparent. If possible, try to read through all the chapters in a section at one sitting. The passages that deal with religious and philosophical ideas demand extra care.

Timeline to Jude the Obscure

Opening of the novel—*Jude is 11*

Jude meets Arabella—*He is 19*

Jude moves to Christminster—*He is 21*

Jude moves to Melchester—*He is 23*

Jude moves to Aldbrickham—*He is 26*

Jude returns to Christminster—*He is 29*

Jude dies—*He is 30*

SECTION TWO

Jude the Obscure

"At Marygreen"

New Characters:

Jude Fawley: *the title character, eleven-year-old orphan who lives with his great-aunt*

Richard Phillotson: *village schoolmaster who is leaving for the university, Jude's early mentor*

Blacksmith and Farm Bailiff: *villagers who help Phillotson move*

Drusilla Fawley: *Jude's great-aunt; she takes in the orphaned Jude and raises him*

Farmer Troutham: *the farmer who catches Jude encouraging birds to eat the grain Jude was supposed to be watching*

Villagers: *people to whom Aunt Drusilla relates Jude's history*

Carter: *a workman who meets Jude on the road*

Two Workmen: *help Jude climb on the roof of a barn to see Christminster*

Physician Vilbert: *the quack doctor who promises and fails to deliver Greek and Latin texts to Jude*

Arabella Donn: *the pig-keeper's daughter; she is Jude's wife*

Mr. and Mrs. Donn: *Arabella's parents*

Anny and Sarah: *Arabella's friends and confidantes*

Mr. Challow: *the pig-killer who arrives late, forcing Jude and Arabella to kill the pig*

Summary

The novel opens with Phillotson's departure from the Marygreen school, where he had been the schoolmaster. Jude is, at the time, eleven years old, and comes to say good-bye. Even at this stage, Jude is considered less worthy of education and has been attending night school. Phillotson tells Jude that he plans on moving to Christminster in order to gain admission and eventually get a degree. This is the first Jude had heard of a university degree.

In Chapter II, the reader learns that Jude's parents are dead and that Jude lives with his great-aunt, Drusilla, a very cynical old woman. She is not happy to have him live with her, but is resigned to doing her duty. He is working for Farmer Troutham, scaring crows from the corn. However, Troutham discovers that Jude is talking to the crows and allowing them to eat corn. Jude is flogged, then fired. Jude's aunt, who already resents his presence, is angry with him. Jude runs off toward Christminster.

Chapter III describes Jude's trip along the road to Christminster, a journey which widens his horizons. With the help of workmen, he climbs up on the roof of a barn in order to catch a glimpse of the city. As he is wont to do, he daydreams as he walks, and imagines seeing Phillotson through a window. As he begins to return to Marygreen, he meets some older men who encourage him by speaking of the glories of the university, most of which they have gleaned from the stories of others. These stories spark Jude's interest in pursuing a scholarly life.

In Chapter IV, he first asks Physician Vilbert to bring him copies of Latin and Greek grammars, but when the doctor forgets, he writes to Phillotson, who has just sent for his piano, and asks for the texts. When they arrive, he attempts to read them; however, he becomes very frustrated as he has difficulty understanding them.

Chapter V takes place three years later, when he has mastered Latin and Greek. He has been helping his aunt with her bakery and also has become apprenticed to a stonemason and church rebuilder, like his uncle whom he never met.

In Chapter VI, as he is walking along ruminating about his plans, Jude is hit by pig flesh thrown from behind a bush. The thrower is Arabella Donn. He makes a date to meet her the next day, though he senses that his attraction to her is rather superficial. Although he is loath to leave his studies, he meets her for tea and a walk in the countryside in Chapter VII, and in Chapter VIII she resolves, on the advice of her friends, to become pregnant, thereby trapping him into marriage.

In Chapter IX, Arabella tells Jude she is pregnant. The villagers say that Jude has compromised himself, and that she is beneath him. However, Jude is resolved to do the right thing. After they quickly marry, she tells him she was mistaken and is not pregnant. He is repulsed when he sees that she wears false hair. It represents, to him, her generally mendacious nature.

In Chapter X, the contrast between Jude and Arabella's attitudes emerges when they must slaughter their pig. When Challow, the pig-killer, is late, the couple set out to do the task themselves so that Jude will not miss work. Jude, who is sensitive to animals, wants to kill the pig humanely while Arabella, the daughter of a pig farmer, wants it to die slowly to improve the quality of the meat. In Chapter XI, Jude and Arabella realize that they are incompatible. She throws his books on the floor and he hits her. While he is out drinking, she departs, leaving a note for Jude that says "Have gone with my friends. Will not be back." Shortly thereafter, she goes with her family to Australia.

Analysis

Marygreen is a provincial town where people are suspicious of the outside world, particularly of Christminster, location of the university. Hardy sees this provincialism as both positive and negative. Many of the problems in the novel are the result of urban influence as much as rural attitudes.

All major characters except Sue Bridehead are introduced in this section, and she is briefly mentioned. In a sense, the groundwork is lain here for Jude's attraction to his cousin. He gains a taste for learning, and becomes dissatisfied with a relationship based solely on physical attraction, which is the basis of his union with Arabella.

Attitudes toward education comprise an important theme of this section. Essentially, a university education was for upper-class males. Most middle-class men did not attend the university, and certainly, the working class did not. The schoolmaster, Phillotson, who will later become a rival, is here a role model for Jude. However, Jude's background does not afford him the same opportunities as Phillotson's does him. From an early age, Jude is expected to perform physical labor. Also, Jude's interest in Christminster is at odds with the attitudes of his aunt and many of the other villagers, who see Christminster as evil.

"At Marygreen" is filled with biblical allusions, the most obvious of which are the choice of the names "Christminster" and "Marygreen" to replace "Oxford" and "Fawley." Christminster comes to represent salvation, first for Phillotson, then for Jude.

Jude longs for a university degree, not for social or financial advancement, but for its own sake, as a sort of holy grail. He sees it as providing spiritual fulfillment; at times his intellectual and religious pursuits seem at odds.

In Chapter III, as Jude walks away from Christminster, he thinks that it takes on a glow, like a halo. He thinks of it as "a city of light" and that "the tree of knowledge" grows there. These references allude to the conflict that Jude soon faces between scholarship and religion. The tree of knowledge led to the fall of man, thereby suggesting Hardy's ambiguous feelings toward university study.

Another theme that Hardy develops in this section is the interaction between man and nature. Jude's love for animals gets him into trouble in a world where animals are seen as existing solely for human use. He allows the crows to eat Farmer Troutham's corn, thereby losing his job, and he is unwilling to cause the pig any pain. As with his intellectual ambitions, Jude's sensitivity evinces his lack of pragmatism.

The characterization of Arabella is another important aspect of this section, not only for her role in the story but for Jude's perception of her. Even by Marygreen's standards she is low-class and considered not good enough for Jude. After they marry, he is disgusted, not only by the trick that she has played on him, but by the fact that she formerly worked as a barmaid and by the false hair that she wears. Both she and Jude long for better things in life,

however, Jude is intellectually and spiritually ambitious while Arabella is money-hungry and socially ambitious.

The discussion of marriage in this section begins to show Hardy's sense of mistrust of the institution. Jude's Aunt Drusilla has never married and she warns Jude in Chapter II that the Fawleys should not marry. This warning almost seems justified in Chapter XI when, as Jude and Arabella argue, Arabella throws Jude's books on the floor and Jude grabs her with some force. She accuses him of abusing her as his mother abused his father. He then goes out and gets drunk. There is a strong sense of fate and cynicism in this situation. Initially, Arabella's friends convinced her to trap Jude by getting pregnant. Her attraction to Jude is genuine, but she easily falls into the role of a shrewish wife, while Jude falls into the role of a drunk and abusive husband.

Study Questions

1. How does Jude learn about the University of Christminster?

2. What is Jude's job at the beginning of the novel? How does he lose it?

3. How does Jude meet Arabella Donn?

4. What are some of the conflicts between Jude and Arabella?

5. What is Aunt Drusilla's attitude toward Jude?

6. What does Christminster represent to Jude?

7. What circumstances shaped the lives of Jude's parents?

8. What books does Jude read?

9. What is the attitude of people in Marygreen toward Christminster?

10. What happened to Jude's parents?

Answers

1. Jude learns of Christminster from the schoolmaster, Richard Phillotson.

2. Jude's job is to scare birds away from Farmer Troutham's corn. He loses his job when the farmer catches him talking to the birds and encouraging the birds to eat the corn.

3. Jude meets Arabella near the riverbank, when she throws pig flesh at him.

4. Jude is more interested in ideas, whereas Arabella is more pragmatic.

5. Aunt Drusilla resents having to care for Jude, but is resigned to his presence.

6. Christminster represents a finer world than the one Jude knows.

7. His parents were unhappily married and poor.

8. Jude reads, among others, Caesar, Virgil, Homer, and the Bible.

9. The villagers of Marygreen are suspicious of Christminster.

10. Jude's parents separated, then died.

Suggested Essay Topics

1. The author represents Jude as a naive young man who is lured into marriage by the more experienced and scheming Arabella. Discuss how the relationship between Jude and Arabella is similar to or different from modern day male-female relationships.

2. Religion and morality are woven through these early chapters, from the name of the university town to the permanence of the marriage bond. Pick several scenes using religious or moral imagery and themes and discuss them.

3. Education is Jude's great goal. What mixture of dreams, escapism, and ambition drive him toward this goal? Discuss.

"At Christminster"

New Characters:

Sue Bridehead: *she marries Phillotson, she is Jude's cousin*

Mrs. Edlin: *friend of Jude's aunt*

Vendor: *sells statues of Apollo and Venus to Sue*

Miss Fontover: *Sue's employer and landlady*

Mrs. Hawes: *Sue's second landlady. Chaperones Phillotson and Sue during tutoring sessions*

John Marygreen: *villager who asks Jude about Christminster*

Uncle Jim, Uncle Joe: *stoneworkers with whom Jude passes time drinking*

Undergraduates: *students who encourage Jude to drunkenly recite Latin in a bar*

Tinker Taylor: *iron worker with whom Jude drinks*

Mr. Highridge: *a curate; comforts Jude and urges him to become a minister*

Nurse: *woman who looks after Jude's great aunt*

Neighbor: *confirms Drusilla's stories about Sue*

Summary

In the opening chapter of this section, Jude moves to Christminster, in part to be near the university which he longs to attend, and in part because his cousin, Sue Bridehead, lives there. They have never met, but Jude has seen her picture at his aunt's house and is curious about her. When he arrives in the town, he finds a room in which to stay. As he walks around Christminster, he imagines the famous people who have studied there. They seem so real to him that he begins to hold conversations with them. When he goes back to his lodging, he dreams of poets and statesmen, but in the end his mind drifts back to Sue.

Jude has finished his apprenticeship, and in Chapter II looks for work as a stonemason. Eventually, he is employed and sets out

to look for his cousin. He finds her working in a shop that sells religious statuary. He considers approaching her but does not. He spends a great deal of time thinking about her and about what establishing contact with her would entail, as he feels himself attracted to her. He is self-conscious of their difference in social status; he is also afraid that if a romantic relationship developed it would be morally questionable, as he considers himself still married to Arabella. Finally, he fears that his aunt may be right, both about Sue's character and about the curse on marriage in both families. However, he sees her several times by chance. In Chapter III, he begins to attend the same church as she does.

Meanwhile, Sue buys statues of the pagan gods Venus and Apollo from a vendor in the countryside. Jude continues to admire Sue from afar when, in Chapter IV, she comes to the stonemason's yard and asks about him. He arranges to meet her, and together they go to see Phillotson. At first, Phillotson does not remember Jude, but eventually he does and he offers Sue, who has previously worked as a teacher, a spot in a training school for teachers.

In Chapter V, Phillotson must give Sue private tutoring, and he begins to fall in love with her. They take their students to see a model of Jerusalem and argue over the relevance of the Holy Land in Christian religious life. When Jude finds out about their relationship, he is very upset. When, in Chapter VI, Jude's aunt becomes ill, he returns to Marygreen to care for her. She and a neighbor tell Jude more about Sue's past—that Sue had always been unconventional and intellectual. Shortly thereafter Jude writes to the university officials regarding admission and is rejected. He is told that a working-class individual is better off sticking to his trade.

In Chapter VII, Jude goes to a pub to drink and forget his problems, he gets involved in a conversation with some Christminster undergraduates. They prod him and he begins to recite in Latin, clearly understanding more than they do. He curses them for their ignorance and runs out of the bar. He goes directly to Sue's and falls asleep in her living room. However, when he awakes, he is ashamed and starts back to Marygreen. Upon arriving, he goes to the church and speaks with Mr. Highridge, the clergyman. Highridge urges him to enter the church, which Jude wishes to do, although he has doubts that he is actually cut out for the ministry.

Analysis

In "At Christminster," the important conflicts of the novel are developed. Jude is denied admission to Christminster and the love triangle of Jude, Sue, and Phillotson begins. Also, Sue Bridehead, one of the most distinctive heroines in nineteenth-century literature, is introduced. She is attractive, intelligent, and unconventional, yet she faces many difficulties and dilemmas.

Sue is categorized by many literary critics as a "New Woman". One of the emerging female types in the late 1800s. This categorization is distinct from that of the feminist. In the 1890s, feminists were individuals who believed in and fought for political and social rights for women. They pushed for suffrage, the right to own property, marital rights, and equality of opportunity. Feminists included women and sympathetic men, such as John Stuart Mill, who worked together to achieve a goal.

New Women, on the other hand, were free spirits. They differed from traditional Victorian women in that they acted on their instincts. They did not see themselves as part of a cause, but as individuals with strong feelings. Independence might be expressed through relationships with several men at the same time.

Jude's and Sue's paths cross several times before they actually meet. Significantly, it is she who makes the first move. He has been hesitant to approach her despite his feeling of desire for her, and to some extent, this reluctance foreshadows the eventual troubles in the relationship.

Clearly, Jude's initial attraction to Sue is physical, as was his attraction to Arabella. Seeing her photograph gives him the desire to meet her. However, before he does so, he has formed a more complete picture through observation. He discovers that she is more than just a pretty girl; her education and talent seem products of the world he aspires to enter.

This section of the novel shows Jude's frustration, not only in terms of his relationship with Sue, but in terms of his inability to fulfill his dreams of an education. His timidity at approaching a man whom he believes to be a provost is similar to his fear of approaching Sue. He is rejected by the university in the same chapter that he learns that Phillotson has fallen in love with Sue. In both these situations, he feels that his working-class background makes him less attractive to those he desires.

Jude's feelings about the university also have a somewhat mystical, religious quality. In his visions, he almost deifies religious scholars whom he admires. His fantasies make accessible to him that which he realistically cannot achieve. While he strives to learn, he lacks the critical perspective which might show him the human, fallible side of his idols.

The religious philosophers admired by Jude are generally of the Tractarian School. This movement sought to resolve the distinction between the Catholic and Anglican churches. Jude is drawn to this movement, not only because of its prevalence in intellectual circles at the time, but because it allows for a more mystical, emotional outlook on religion. Major figures in the Tractarian movement were Cardinal Newman, John Keble, Edward Pusey, and William Ward.

Sue's religious views differ from the traditional, although she veers in the opposite direction. She prefers the ancient civilizations of Greece and Rome to the Holy Land, as is evident in her choice of statuary. She believes that the Holy Land has little significance in modern life. Her argument with Phillotson over the importance of the Holy Land shows her willingness to question authority. In her theological tendencies, Sue is along the lines of Puritans and other dissenters, opposing a highly structured church.

Even before he actually applies for admission to the university, Jude, for a moment, doubts his own quest for education. His love for Sue seems a worthy substitute, but also he feels, at times, that the trade in which he has been trained and at which he excels is as significant as university study. When the letter arrives rejecting him, saying that he is better off as a stonemason, he does not disagree entirely with its contents.

One might expect someone in his position who has longed fervently for an education to fight the university's rejection, but he accepts it fatalistically.

The issue of the permanence of marriage is also raised frequently in "At Christminster". Jude feels that somehow, even though Arabella left him, he is still her husband. Also, his marriage to Arabella has left him cynical about such a relationship. He suspects

that the problems between them may not just be those of personality and goals, but the result of a problem with the institution of marriage.

There is a sharp contrast between Hardy's view of marriage as expressed through Jude and that of earlier Victorian novelists such as Charlotte Brontë. In *Jane Eyre*, the novel ends happily with Jane's marriage. Even Hardy's earlier novels, such as *Far from the Madding Crowd*, portrayed marriage in a more positive light. Possibly Hardy's difficulties with his own first marriage are reflected in the lives of his characters.

Throughout the novel, there is an important contrast between Jude and Phillotson. On the one hand, Phillotson has served as a role model for Jude and on the other, he becomes a rival. Phillotson, too, is somewhat frustrated with his life, having not achieved his goal of becoming a parson. Jude, in seeking out the schoolmaster, has created the situation in which the object of his affections chooses someone else. His idealism and propensity to worship others have caused him to betray his own desire.

Hence in all areas of his life, Jude feels great trepidation and uncertainty. Psychologically speaking, the loss of both his parents at an early age, as well as his aunt's coldness, might create these feelings. However, Hardy clearly intends that Jude be a reflection of his times as well. The late Victorian Age lacked the confidence of the earlier part of the era. The negative effects of industrialization were beginning to reach the countryside. To some extent, Jude is ahead of his time, as is Sue, but in another sense he is deeply tied to the past.

Jude has been trained to reconstruct Gothic, medieval churches. Hardy placed great value in historical preservation, believing urbanization to be the source of the destruction of the rural past. To some extent, Hardy's commentary on this is tangential to the plot; the contrast between country and city is also evident in the relationship between Jude and Sue. Hardy's father was a church rebuilder, and Hardy himself was trained as an architect. He imbues Jude with the same sort of love for old churches that he feels.

Study Questions

1. Where does Sue Bridehead work?

2. Why does Sue want to leave Christminster?

3. What is the difference between a feminist and a New Woman?

4. Why is Jude hesitant to approach Sue?

5. How does Sue react to Phillotson's advances?

6. What happens when Jude drinks with undergraduates in a bar?

7. How does Jude first learn of Sue's existence?

8. To how many academic dignitaries does Jude write?

9. What kind of job does Jude get for Sue?

10. At the end of "At Christminster," what does Jude think about doing?

Answers

1. Sue works in a shop that sells religious statues.

2. She plans to leave Christminster because her landlady smashed her statues of Venus and Apollo.

3. A feminist believed in rights for women. A New Woman rebelled by expressing her individuality even if it defied convention.

4. Jude is afraid that he is, in fact, still married and that any relationship is bound to turn out badly, in part because of the supposed hereditary curse on his family.

5. She neither encourages nor discourages him.

6. Jude recites in Latin, then curses the undergraduates for their ignorance.

7. Jude sees the picture of Sue that his great-aunt has.

8. Jude writes to five academic dignitaries.

9. Jude gets Sue a job as a schoolteacher working for Phillotson.

10. Jude considers entering the Church.

Suggested Essay Topics

1. Discuss Hardy's portrayal of the university. Use examples from the novel.

2. Both Jude and Phillotson attend the University in the hopes of advancing intellectually. Things did not turn out the way they had originally planned. Discuss the different ways in which these two characters deal with the hand they are dealt. How could the novel have been different?

3. Discuss Hardy's treatment of marriage and romantic love in this section. Why did he treat his characters in that way? Do you agree or disagree with his treatment of marriage and love?

4. Characters in *Jude the Obscure* have different views about religion. Contrast the various views on religion expressed in "At Christminster". Can there be one "right" view of religion? Explain.

"At Melchester"

New Characters:

Shepherd and his Mother: *country people who invite Sue and Jude to spend the night in their home*

Students at Sue's College: *busybodies who spread rumors about Sue after she spends the night away from school*

Miss Traceley: *school official whose duties include roll call*

Porter: *the school worker who hears splashing in the river*

Mr. Cockman: *flirts with Arabella*

The Undergraduate: *deceased student with whom Sue had a long intellectual relationship*

The Musician: *author of a piece of religious music; he rejects Jude because he is poor*

Jude's Landlady: *the landlady at Melchester*

Minister: *marries Sue and Phillotson*

Summary

Once again, in Chapter I, Jude makes plans to move to be near Sue. She is entering a training college for teachers at Melchester. Jude decides to apply to the Theological College at Melchester. He has recast his ambitions and decided that to be a threadbare village curate is a more noble goal than that of becoming a scholar. However, while he is saving up the money to do this, Sue writes to him to say that she is miserable and asking that he come see her. When he arrives, she tells him that Phillotson has asked her to marry him in two years' time. Although Jude is upset, he finds a place to stay and a job repairing cathedrals.

In Chapter II, Jude and Sue set out on a walk in the country. They wander farther than they intend and miss the train. A shepherd lets them spend the night in his cottage. Chapter III begins with Sue missing her curfew. The mistress discovers her absence. When Sue returns, she is punished by being confined to her room. However, she escapes and goes to Jude's lodgings.

Then, in Chapter IV, Sue tells Jude of her experience in London where she shared an apartment with an undergraduate. He taught her much, but became ill and died. Sue has, however, maintained her virginity, as she fears giving another power over her. She speaks of her disdain for Christminster, which she feels is merely an organ of Anglicanism. The discussion becomes heated when Jude expresses a view of religion more conservative than Sue's. Sue clearly wishes to alter Jude's views so that they conform to her own.

At the beginning of Chapter V, Sue departs for Shaston, intending to stay with a friend. She fears that the training college will not allow her to return. After she tells Jude not to love her, she quickly sends him a letter rescinding the admonition. Upon his return to Shaston, she reveals that she has been expelled from the training college and told that she ought to marry as soon as possible to avoid further damage to her reputation. She will probably marry Phillotson, since Jude waited too long to declare his feelings for her. Again, he leaves feeling put off, only to receive a letter shortly thereafter apologizing for the rejection.

In Chapter VI, Phillotson also moves to Shaston, where he was born, and sets up a school. He is very much in love with Sue, and his discovery that she has been expelled from the training school

upsets him tremendously. Finding Jude in the stonemason's yard,
he asks him about the incident. Jude essentially tells him the truth.

Jude then finds Sue and tells her of his previous marriage to
Arabella. Sue is at first suspicious, but eventually she accepts Jude's
explanation.

In Chapter VII, Sue writes Jude that she and Phillotson are to
be married shortly. She requests that Jude give her away. Though
deeply hurt, he complies. He and Sue rehearse the ceremony together and Jude buys Sue a wedding present. The wedding takes
place and the wedding party returns to Jude's lodgings for a meal.
As Sue and Phillotson are getting into the carriage to leave, Sue
realizes that she has forgotten her handkerchief. She runs back into
the house to get it and seems close to confiding something to Jude,
but says nothing and goes with her husband.

Chapter VIII finds Jude returning to Marygreen to see his aunt,
whose condition has worsened. While there, he takes a trip to
Christminster where he runs into Arabella, who is a barmaid. She
has returned from Australia where she was briefly married to another man. Jude expresses his disapproval, but they spend the night
together.

Subsequently, in Chapter IX Jude sees Sue by chance. She has
also come to see Aunt Drusilla, so they visit her together. Sue questions her aunt about reasons that one might marry. When Aunt
Drusilla replies that it is wrong to marry someone one does not
love, Sue runs out of the room crying, realizing that is what she has
done. She then returns to Shaston. Jude receives a letter from
Arabella saying that her Australian husband has come to England
and that she will go off with him.

Jude returns to Melchester in Chapter X, having decided he
lacks the temperament for the clergy. He does sing in the church
choir and when he hears a hymn he particularly likes, he goes to
Kennetbridge to tell the composer how much he likes his work.
The composer is responsive until he realizes that Jude doesn't have
money, at which point he treats Jude coldly. He himself has decided that there is no money in music and plans to go into the wine
business. He had hoped that Jude would be a potential customer.
Disillusioned, Jude writes to Sue, asking if he might visit her. She
agrees to let him visit.

Analysis

The most important development in this section is probably the description of Sue's views both on religion and on relationships between men and women, and her revelations of past experience. The character of Sue Bridehead is largely responsible for the controversy surrounding *Jude the Obscure*, whether or not her views mirrored Hardy's views.

First, her relationship with the undergraduate shocked many nineteenth-century readers. The fact that she kept her virginity probably had little mitigating value. It was the appearance of illicit activity, as much as the actual activity, that bothered Victorians, as Sue discovers when she is expelled from the training college. Sue's preservation of her virginity does, however, demonstrate the limitations on the literalness of her outlook. Her rebellion is highly cerebral—she cannot commit herself physically to her beliefs.

Second, Sue is clearly intellectually superior to Jude, thereby violating the conventions of the time. It is she who controls the conversation, and she who wishes to educate him. Also, she is of the middle class, and it was considered inappropriate for someone of her status to marry a working-class man.

The restrictions typically placed on young Victorian women are depicted in Chapter III, where Hardy gives a poignant description of the training college which Sue attends. Aged nineteen to twenty-one, the women are prohibited from seeing men, and the overall atmosphere is highly repressive. Hardy makes it clear that the women are restricted, not as a function of social class—as they come from a range of backgrounds—but as a result of gender.

The handicap Jude endures for his working-class status is, however, not entirely unlike the oppression felt by women. Women too, had few opportunities to study at the university level. The common feeling of oppression is another factor that unites Jude and Sue. They must find ways around social norms rather than fitting into them.

The issue of social class is evident in Jude's encounter with the musician in Chapter X. Even an artist is motivated by money and is unreceptive to praise from someone poor. The pattern has clearly developed wherein Jude develops an attraction to something that he cannot achieve or possess due to social and economic status.

The other effect of class barriers in the novel is the difficulty of marriage between members of different classes. Sue's initial choice of Phillotson, over Jude, results at least in part from Phillotson's middle-class status, whereas both Jude and Arabella would be considered working class.

In addition to her actions, Sue's opinions distinguish her from other young women. While Jude is attracted to the somewhat controversial, but conservative, Tractarian Movement, Sue insists on an individualistic reading of the Bible. Whereas Jude relies heavily on the church, Sue rebels against organized religion. Jude has somewhat conservative morals. Paradoxically, he passes harsher judgment on Sue's past than does Phillotson.

Sue and Jude also disagree in their views of the university. Despite his rejection, Jude remains worshipful, whereas Sue is skeptical and critical. This is based, in part, on her rejection of the Anglican Church, which she sees as a controlling influence at Christminster. It is also based on her reading of Edward Gibbon, a politician and historian who harshly critiqued Oxford. An interesting contrast develops between Sue and Arabella which parallels, to some extent, the contrast between Jude and Phillotson. Each woman represents a different side of Jude. Arabella is largely a negative character, but in the end she survives. She is pragmatic and able to operate within social boundaries. She essentially commits bigamy, but is not so severely punished as Sue is for merely spending the night in the same house with Jude. This discrepancy results from Arabella's willingness to stay within the confines of her social role. She is ambitious, but does not attempt to transcend gender and social class. Arabella knows that sex and money are interconnected, and so she is economically motivated. She does not concern herself with ideology, as Sue does.

To some extent, Phillotson, too, does not equivocate and straightforwardly tells Sue his feelings, whereas Jude fears such revelation. Jude also argues with Sue, and judges her rather than taking charge of the situation as Phillotson does. Like Arabella, he takes the more pragmatic course. However, his social position allows him to do so, in that he offers Sue some social acceptability. Sue clearly feels the conflict between her feelings for Jude and her desire for social respectability. Arabella and Sue present Jude with a dichotomy;

Jude and Phillotson create such a conflict for Sue. Phillotson represents social acceptability, whereas Jude represents love and friendship, as well as being a receptive listener for her ideas.

Aunt Drusilla is a relatively minor character. However, she is the link between Sue and Jude. There is little in *Jude* about a traditional nuclear family. The characters seem to be set apart, to live in something of a vacuum. For a long time Jude knows only Aunt Drusilla, who is not even an aunt, but a great-aunt. Sue, also, has no one else after her father dies. Even Arabella has a stepmother rather than a natural mother. In part, Hardy portrays this lack of connectedness in a positive light. The characters are freer to follow their hearts. No parent is controlling them. Arabella and Phillotson do have more of a support system—Arabella consults Anny and Phillotson consults Gillingham. However, this consultation is depicted somewhat unfavorably, as the characters are influenced into taking cruel actions. In the end, however, the absence of family will also have dire consequences.

The severed family is a common theme in Victorian novels. Orphaned characters are led by providence to lost relatives. This is not the first Hardy novel to deal with such a theme; *Tess of the D'Urbervilles* involves the discovery of rich relatives. However, in *Tess*, and eventually in *Jude*, the families are not successfully rejoined. Outside influences are stronger than familial ties.

Study Questions

1. What type of ruins do Jude and Sue go see?
2. Whose pictures does Sue have at the training school?
3. What does the school think has happened to Sue after she escapes?
4. What happened to Sue's friend from London?
5. What does Sue leave behind after her wedding?
6. With whom is Arabella talking when Jude sees her?
7. To which nineteenth-century philosopher does Jude compare Sue?
8. What does Jude give Sue as a wedding present?

9. What happens to the money that the undergraduate leaves Sue?

10. Why does Sue dislike Christminster?

Answers

1. Jude and Sue go to see the Corinthian Ruins.

2. Sue has pictures of the undergraduate and of Phillotson.

3. The school thinks that Sue may have drowned.

4. Sue's friend has died.

5. Sue leaves behind her handkerchief.

6. Arabella is talking with Mr. Cockman, an undergraduate.

7. Jude compares Sue to Voltaire.

8. Jude gives Sue yards of white tulle.

9. Sue loses the money in a bubble scheme.

10. Sue dislikes Christminster because she considers it an organ of the Anglican Church.

Suggested Essay Topics

1. Sue speaks with extreme bitterness when she discusses religion, marriage, and Christminster. Pick several examples of her views on these subjects and analyze what she means by her statements and why she feels the way she does.

2. Arabella is presented as coarse and crude, yet she seems to be free of the tortured conflicts that are making Jude and Sue nervous. Discuss the costs and benefits of chasing after material success as Arabella does and waging the struggles that consume Jude and Sue.

3. Sue is portrayed as weak, unable to stick to her principles and involved in a marriage not founded on love. Discuss how social convention limited women's lives during the time portrayed in the book.

"At Shaston"

New Characters:

Gillingham: *Phillotson's childhood friend, he offers comfort when Sue leaves*

Waiting Maid: *hotel staff member who tells Sue that Jude was there with Arabella*

Chairman of the School Committee: *demands that Phillotson resign after Sue leaves*

Itinerants: *people who defend Phillotson at his public hearing*

Summary

"At Shaston" begins with a description of the town, remote and known for its wantonness. Jude arrives to visit Sue and together they play hymns on the same piano that Phillotson had at Marygreen. Both are moved by the music and their hands clasp. They discuss religious views again. Jude is interested in learning more about the New Testament. Sue recommends that he read Cowper's *Apocryphal Gospels*. Sue also confides in Jude that she is not entirely happy in her marriage. Before Jude leaves Shaston for Melchester, he walks past the house where Sue and Phillotson live and watches them through the window.

In Chapter II, Sue writes to Jude, telling him not to visit again as their flirtation is dangerous for a married woman. Then, Aunt Drusilla dies and Jude and Sue see each other at the funeral. Sue complains to Jude, relating her dissatisfaction with her marriage. He informs her that he plans to go back to Arabella. As she continues to bemoan her fate, they embrace.

In Chapter III, Sue kisses Jude good-bye as she leaves for Shaston. This is their first real kiss. Jude subsequently burns all of his religious books. When she arrives home, Sue tells Phillotson, after some discussion, that she wishes to leave him and live with Jude. She quotes John Stuart Mill, to which Phillotson replies: "What do I care about Mill?" At school the next day, they exchange notes in which Sue confirms her desire to leave him and he expresses his regret, but agrees to think about it. She begins to live in another part of the house.

At the beginning of Chapter IV, Phillotson discovers that Sue has jumped out of a second-story window, nearly injuring herself in an attempt to escape. The next evening, Phillotson goes to see his friend Gillingham, who tells him he is crazy to consider letting Sue go. However, when he returns home, he tells Sue that she may leave.

In Chapter VI, Sue joins Jude, and they decide to move to Aldbrickham to avoid scandal. Phillotson faces such a scandal in Chapter VII. When the head of the school discovers that Sue has left and that Phillotson did nothing to prevent her, he is fired and ostracized, although some itinerants in the town support him, as does Gillingham. He falls ill and Sue comes to see him. Still, Phillotson does not try to win her back.

Analysis

No town in the novel, except perhaps Christminster, is described with such detail and vividness as Shaston. On the whole, Hardy gives far less description of the landscape than he has done in other novels. However, he does not omit description here. Hardy may have done this to create a contrast between Shaston and the towns where Jude previously lived. He also may have wished to establish the importance of sensory perception at this stage of the novel. Jude has put aside both scholarship and religion, and becomes driven by desire. Shaston's remoteness may be particularly significant and warrant more descriptive detail because it serves as a metaphor for Jude's "obscurity."

As in the rest of the novel, light—of both candles and the sun—is an important image. It can be either warm and inviting or forbidding and vengeful. The evening light creates an atmosphere conducive to the romantic encounter in the Shaston schoolhouse. When Phillotson leaves his house to see Gillingham, the lights in the windows seem to be watching him. When he is ill, he sees the sunset as "tongues of fire." Light is symbolic both of religious enlightenment and human affection. As in the rest of the novel, there is constant interplay and conflict between religion and sexual attraction.

Jude and Sue are brought together by a common interest in religion, yet it would be impossible for the relationship, at least from Jude's perspective, to be seen in asexual terms. They do not, however, find a place for their relationship within the contemporary religious and social scheme.

The major event that takes place in "At Shaston," Phillotson's agreement that Sue may leave to live with Jude, is somewhat remarkable for people of the middle class in rural England. First, Sue is planning to live with a man out of wedlock. Second, Phillotson, though he wants Sue, does not try to enforce his claim on her. To an extent, Phillotson takes an attitude similar to Sue's in his willingness to live outside the rules.

The earlier break-up of Jude and Arabella does not cause a scandal, basically because of the low social status of the characters. The split of a barmaid and a stonemason does not have the same effect as that of two teachers. Entry into the middle class leads to a sacrifice of freedom.

There is a paradox in the scandal caused by Sue in that she is anything but sexually wanton. She holds back both from Jude and Phillotson, as she did with the undergraduate in London. Many readers have considered her a tease, even cruel. She manipulates Jude by allowing him "just one kiss" and admonishing him not to love her. When Sue leaves Phillotson, although Phillotson believes that she and Jude will live together as man and wife, she does not immediately consent to sexual relations with Jude. She is disturbed when she finds that they are going to the same hotel where Jude stayed with Arabella, and refuses to do so.

Sue's departure from Phillotson is certainly precipitated by the death of Aunt Drusilla. An impediment to Jude and Sue's relationship has been removed, but so has a link. The loss of the sense of cousinship creates a vacuum, a need for a sexual connection.

Phillotson's character is an important issue in the surprising turn of events. A more passionate person would not have allowed Sue her freedom. Like Sue, however, he is ruled first by ideas. Her decision to marry him was made rationally, rather than emotionally; his decision to let her go is the product of reason. He is objective enough to recognize the affection between Jude and Sue, and to see that his own relationship with Sue cannot match it.

At the beginning of the novel, Phillotson encouraged Jude to pursue an education; he was a father figure to Jude. However, it

was Jude who introduced Sue to him. This relationship is an important dynamic in the story. He does not seem to hate Jude, at this point, and it is probably this lack of animosity that enables him to let Sue go.

The role of Phillotson's friend, Gillingham, is to tell Phillotson the opinion that the average person will have about his decision to let Sue leave. It does not seem that he is married, yet he holds a traditional, male-centered view of marriage. He comes to understand his friend's view, but he does not share it.

Music plays a role in this section, as it did at the end of "At Melchester". Both Jude and Sue are greatly moved by the hymn Jude plays. It is the hymn written by the composer whom he had approached. This enables Jude to transcend the composer's rejection and, in fact, begins the physical relationship between Jude and Sue. While they have different backgrounds and conflicting ideas and tastes, music is a common ground. Music had, of course, played an important role in Hardy's own upbringing.

Illness, too, is an important theme here, and throughout the novel. Unnamed illnesses seem to be depressions. Sue becomes "ill" when she leaves the training college and Phillotson becomes "ill" when Sue leaves. Sickness provides a reason for visits that would otherwise be inappropriate. Aunt Drusilla's illness and death bring Jude and Sue together.

The poet mentioned most frequently in *Jude* is Percy Bysshe Shelley. Jude and Sue quote him to each other, and Phillotson tells Gillingham that Jude and Sue remind him of Laon and Cythna, lovers from Shelley's "The Revolt of Islam." This long poem is an imaginary version of the French Revolution, set in Asia. Laon and Cythna are brother and sister who commit incest and have a child. Sue asks Jude to recite lines from "Epipsychidion," Shelley's wedding ode. Shelley is an apt muse for the novel, both in the romantic nature of his work and in the rebellious nature of his life. His skepticism appeals to Sue.

Another interest common to several characters in *Jude* is the search for meaning in classical antiquity. Phillotson studies Roman ruins, Sue collects pagan statues; Jude reads Greek. Like Walter Pater, a major Victorian writer and art critic, they attempt to define and utilize the past.

Study Questions

1. What are some of the features that distinguish Shaston from the other towns where Jude has lived?

2. What book do Jude and Sue discuss when they first meet in Shaston?

3. What does Sue give Jude when he visits her?

4. What nineteenth-century English philosopher does Sue quote when she is asking Phillotson to let her go with Jude?

5. Why does Phillotson allow Sue to leave?

6. How does Phillotson feel about Sue leaving?

7. How does Sue find out that Jude stayed at the same hotel with Arabella?

8. Why does Jude burn his books?

9. Why does Sue go back to visit Phillotson?

10. What is Phillotson's hobby?

Answers

1. Shaston is remote and known for its seediness.

2. Jude and Sue discuss Cowper's *Apocryphal Gospels*.

3. Sue gives Jude a photograph of herself.

4. Sue quotes J. S. Mill.

5. He allows Sue to leave as an act of generosity because he believes it is the right thing to do.

6. He does not want her to go, but does not wish to hold her against her will.

7. The maid tells Sue that Jude was previously there with Arabella.

8. He burns his books because he does not wish to be a hypocrite.

9. She goes back to visit Phillotson because she feels guilty and worried.

10. Phillotson collects Roman antiquities.

Suggested Essay Topics

1. Why does Sue wish to leave Phillotson? Does Phillotson do the right thing? Does Sue do the right thing? Discuss, using examples from the text.

2. Compare the marriage of Phillotson and Sue with that of Jude and Arabella. In what ways are they similar? How are they different? Which marriage (if any) do you think could succeed and why?

3. Phillotson's friend objects at first to the plan to let Sue leave because such arrangements would mean the end of society life as we know it. This viewpoint is still heard today in discussions of public policy, family life, and social structure. Discuss.

4. When they are back at Marygreen Sue and Jude are kept awake by the shrieks of a rabbit caught in a trap. The author's description of the creature's suffering is detailed. Why does Hardy include this in the novel? Could the animal's entrapment be a metaphor for how Jude and Sue feel trapped by social convention and rules? Write an essay exploring this scene.

"At Aldbrickham and Elsewhere"

New Characters:

Mr. Carlett: *Arabella's second husband*

Little Father Time (Jude, Jr.): *Jude's son by Arabella; he comes to live with Jude and Sue*

Guard: *attendant on train carrying Little Father Time to Aldbrickham*

Working Woman and Other Passengers: *Little Father Time's companions on the trip to Aldbrickham*

Collector: *directs Little Father Time to Jude's house*

Three Brides and Bridegrooms: *Jude and Sue observe their weddings at registry and church*

Witness and Others: *watch wedding in registry; tell Jude and Sue about bride and groom*

Clerk: *marries couples at registry*

Messenger: *informs Jude of a job at the church in Aldbrickham*

Old Vicar and Churchwarden: *observe Jude's work; are surprised that Sue is helping him. Churchwarden tells a story about painting commandments*

Charwomen and Two Ladies: *gossip about Sue's marital status*

Willis: *contractor who hires Jude to work on the church; fires him because of relationship with Sue*

Auctioneer: *sells Jude's and Sue's belongings*

Summary

In Chapter I of this section, Jude and Sue have moved into a house in Aldbrickham and are both attempting to secure divorces from their previous spouses. Jude is eager for them to marry but Sue is uncertain. One day, in Chapter II, when Jude is not home, Arabella comes by seeking money, as her husband has abandoned her. She does not reveal her identity, but Sue suspects that it is Arabella. Arabella returns and speaks to Jude, but Sue will not let her in the house. Against Sue's wishes, Jude goes after Arabella, but cannot find her. He comes back for his boots, because it is raining and he wants to continue searching. Sue begs him not to go back out and she says she'll marry him. He stays and they plan their wedding.

In Chapter III, Jude learns from Arabella that she gave birth to his child eight months after leaving him. The child looks strangely old. He has been living with Arabella's parents, but they can no longer care for him, so he comes to live with Jude and Sue.

In Chapter IV, Jude and Sue learn that the boy is nicknamed "Little Father Time" due to his appearance. For the sake of the child, Sue agrees to marriage. Widow Edlin comes from Marygreen to serve as a witness. She tells more stories of the marital problems of Jude's and Sue's ancestors. One of Jude's ancestors had split with his wife and subsequently their child died. In an effort to steal the

child's coffin for burial with his family, he was caught and hanged for burglary. Widow Edlin ascribes this incident to bad luck. Little Father Time, vexed by the story, urges Jude and Sue not to marry.

While waiting at the registry to be married, Jude and Sue observe the wedding of another couple. The bride and groom appear unhappy. Sue feels uneasy, so they go to the church to be married. Again, they observe a less than enthusiastic pair, so Sue again has doubts and calls it off. They continue to live together.

Chapter V takes place at an agriculture fair attended by Arabella and Carlett, her husband who has returned to her. They spot Jude and Sue, who have made a model of Christminster which they are showing at an art exhibit, and Arabella begins to speak about how odd a couple they make. She shares her feelings with her friend Anny and with Physician Vilbert, who sells her a love potion that she plans to use to get Jude back.

Jude and Sue are the subject of more gossip in Chapter VI. Little Father Time is teased at school for living with a "nominal mother" and Jude is fired from his job at a church after the Churchwarden sees them working together. They sell their furniture and move on to Kennetsbridge.

Chapter VII takes place three years later in Kennetsbridge at another fair, where Sue runs into Arabella again. Arabella has been widowed and Sue now has two children of her own. She tells Arabella that Jude is unwell. At the time of the conversation, Sue is selling cakes shaped like buildings at Christminster. This is the business that she and Jude have set up.

Arabella, in Chapter VII, has ostensibly become religious, and meets her friend Anny for the opening of a new church headed by a preacher from London. She is still somewhat in love with Jude, and seeing Sue has rekindled her interest.

As Arabella and Anny go toward Marygreen, they see Phillotson and offer him a ride. Arabella recognizes Phillotson and tells him that she was once married to Jude. She also convincingly implies that Sue is not doing well, and tells him that he has "the law of Moses on his side." The narrative then shifts back to Sue who is disheartened by her encounter with Arabella. She returns home from the fair to find that Jude has decided that he wants to move the family back to Christminster.

Analysis

At this point in the novel, various threads begin to come together. Little Father Time's childhood recalls Jude's own in that he has lived with relatives, away from his parents. As Jude did, he seems somewhat alien and apart from his surroundings.

The name Little Father Time results from the child's prematurely old appearance. He has seen more of the world and has a perspective that Jude and Sue lack. He is, like both Jude and Sue, hypersensitive, as can be seen in his apprehension at Jude and Sue's decision to marry.

The child has the effect of eliciting passion within Sue, as do her encounters with Arabella. When Jude suggests moving to London, she does not want to, since that is where Arabella lives. She begins to be able to show a sense of possessiveness with regard to Jude, whereas before she seemed other-worldly and cerebral.

Much of "At Aldbrickham" focuses on the interplay between Sue and Arabella. Initially, it is Sue who feels jealous and threatened by Arabella's appearance, but paradoxically, once Arabella's husband returns, it is she who becomes possessive. She tells her husband that the child is still rightfully hers even though he lives with Jude and Sue. Arabella's tendency to follow Sue will continue through the end of the novel.

Aside from feelings for Jude, other superficial similarities between Sue and Arabella appear. Unlike Jude, both have spent time in London. Also, both have a sense of skepticism that Jude lacks. Their goals and motives, however, remain substantially distinct. Arabella aims for social acceptance, whereas Sue tries to break free from social restrictions, although she fears social disapproval.

Arabella and Sue are thrown together, now not just by involvement with Jude, but by Little Father Time. Not only is Sue raising Arabella's son, but as she and Jude are cousins, Arabella and Sue now have a common relative. The child plays a role not unlike that of Aunt Drusilla, in that he warns against the marriage of Jude and Sue, and has a basically cynical outlook.

Within the novel there are several weddings in addition to Jude and Sue's aborted attempts—the weddings they observe. None of these ceremonies are especially happy and all seem to confirm Widow Edlin's statement that "Weddings be funerals."

Jude and Sue's attempts at marriage seem the culmination of Sue's fears about marriage. She cannot stand to think of losing her individuality and falling into the prescribed role of wife as she had ostensibly done with Phillotson. Particularly to Sue, the couples she and Jude observe speak ill of marriage. Neither party in each wedding seems pleased with the other. The debate between Jude and Sue that follows is central to the theme of marriage within the novel. Underlying the debate seems to be Sue's fear that marriage to Jude will be no different than being wed to Phillotson. She states that she would be different from the brides that she sees, but this assertion lacks confidence.

The wrestling over the issue of marriage that takes place in *Jude the Obscure* is in a larger sense a function of the definition of the self which takes place throughout the nineteenth century.

Jude and Sue are not so much concerned with the legal and social institution as with the effect of the institution on their inner lives. For Jude, Arabella destroys the boundaries of his fragile self, and Phillotson does much the same to Sue. For a brief time, while Jude and Sue are together, they feel themselves, and others believe them to be, "two in one. " They are so much in harmony as to have the same self. Paradoxically, this is ideally the aim of marriage, but from Hardy's cynical vantage point, the effect is to the contrary.

The other pivotal events of "At Aldbrickham" are the Great Wessex Agricultural fair and the Kennetsbridge fair. These are microcosms of the rural community. The first fair shows the juxtaposition of the two couples, while at the second, only Arabella and Sue meet. This difference signals the breakdown of the experiment that Jude and Sue have made. The talk of the neighbors inhibits Jude and Sue's public appearance as a couple.

Physician Vilbert represents the superstitious mentality that controls the rural people. Like the belief in the curse on Jude's and Sue's families, these superstitions are so real that they become self-fulfilling prophecies. In the end, both the curse and the love potion will seem genuine.

Jude the Obscure is full of numerous old women who are observers as well as enforcers of social norms. Widow Edlin is one such character whose views are not so harsh as those of the charwomen and the landladies. She is, on the whole, a neutral figure who eventually becomes sympathetic to Sue and Jude.

The focus of the novel has moved from Jude's theoretical pondering to the intellectual and emotional discourse of Jude and Sue, and is now on the practical consequences of Jude's and Sue's relationship. This change is reflected in the shift of narrative perspective to Arabella. The reader is asked to look at Jude and Sue through her eyes.

To an extent, Arabella's perspective mirrors popular opinion. Certainly, the townspeople, both in Aldbrickham and Shaston, are almost a character in the novel. Their views are usually stated briefly by one person, but their force is great. Sue cannot anticipate the problems that living with Jude out of wedlock will cause, although she has lived with an undergraduate in London. Here emerges a distinction between country and city: a different set of morals applies, particularly for women.

The antagonism Jude and Sue feel from the townspeople, like the opposition Phillotson experiences, evokes the ideas of John Stuart Mill in "On Liberty." Mill is quoted throughout the novel; he wrote about the dangers of the tyranny of the majority. He feared the abrogation of the rights of the individual. While no physical or legal force is taken against these characters, they are socially and economically penalized for their unwillingness to conform.

At this stage, Sue's hesitance regarding marriage seems almost self-indulgent and certainly foolish, considering its disastrous consequences. It will become increasingly difficult to sympathize with her position. Hardy is criticizing the narrow-mindedness and hypocrisy of the townspeople, but he also seems to be suggesting that Sue's views are extreme. It seems that if Sue had been able to make the concession of simply marrying Jude, whom she does in fact love, she would face fewer problems. If Sue had more faith in Jude's love for her and agreed to move to London, even though Arabella was there at the time, the couple might have faced less criticism.

As in other sections of the novel, biblical language appears frequently. The allusions usually are made by Jude. Interestingly, he is not phased by the diversion of his lifestyle from the Anglican interpretation of the Bible. The townspeople of Aldbrickham, however, see a discrepancy. It is considered inappropriate for Jude to paint the ten commandments on the wall, as he is committing adultery and thus breaking a commandment. The story the

Churchwarden tells in Chapter VI about the scandal created by commandments being left incomplete without the "Nots" is a satirical commentary on the importance of the letter, rather than the spirit, of the law in the minds of the townspeople. Sue's inference that the sight of the couple brought the story to mind proves correct.

Arabella also mentions the commandments when she tells Phillotson that he "has the law of Moses on his side." Placing these words in the mouth of Arabella is Hardy's way of demonstrating the way in which such words can be twisted. This distortion refers back to the opening quote of the book, which is "The letter killeth." This is from Corinthians, and suggests the danger of literal interpretation.

Animal imagery is evident, as it has been throughout the novel. Sue's release of the pigeons echoes Jude's feeding of the birds at the beginning of the novel and his reluctance to kill the pig. To Sue, the sale of the pigeons is not unlike marriage—she cannot go through with it. After observing the church wedding, Sue comments that the flowers held by the bride are like those placed on a sacrificed heifer. Both Jude and Sue identify with animals and cannot stand to see them in pain. They see their own suffering reflected in the suffering of animals. The hunger of the birds is symbolic of Jude's spiritual and emotional hunger. One night, Jude puts a rabbit caught in a trap out of its misery. For him, marriage to Arabella is a similar type of trap. A comparison is also made between Little Father Time and a kitten carried by a woman in the carriage that brings the child to Aldbrickham. The child, however, lacks the kitten's playful nature, and thus is unable to appreciate the kitten as the other passengers are.

Hardy's use of animal imagery stems, in part, from his interest in the evolutionary theories of Charles Darwin. He considered himself to be one of the early readers of Darwin. That man had descended from animals made the suffering of animals more pitiable, as it was not unlike human suffering.

The effects of the encroaching urban culture can be seen in "At Aldbrickham" and throughout the novel. Sue's ideas are developed in London; even Arabella returns from London with newfound evangelism. The preacher who has come to the countryside represents the usurpation of the country institution by urban sophistication.

Study Questions

1. What do Arabella and Vilbert discuss at the agricultural show?

2. What is Jude working on in the church at Aldbrickham?

3. How does Jude discover that he has a son?

4. How does Little Father Time come to live with Jude and Sue?

5. Why was Little Father Time not christened?

6. What does Sue do with her pigeons?

7. Where is Jude when Arabella first comes to visit him at Aldbrickham?

8. What story does Widow Edlin tell on the night before Jude's and Sue's wedding?

9. Why was Jude fired from his job at the church?

10. What do Jude and Sue sell at the auction?

Answers

1. Arabella and Vilbert discuss the relationship between Jude and Sue.

2. Jude is working on the ten commandments.

3. Arabella sends him a letter telling him he has a son.

4. Little Father Time lives with Jude and Sue when neither Arabella or her parents want the responsibility of caring for him.

5. He says he was not christened so his family would be spared the cost of a Christian burial.

6. Sue releases the pigeons after they are sold.

7. Jude is at a history lecture.

8. Widow Edlin tells the story of the failed marriages of some of Jude's and Sue's ancestors.

9. He was fired because a contractor heard vicious gossip about him.

10. Jude and Sue sell their furniture, including that which he inherited from Great-Aunt Drusilla.

Suggested Essay Topics

1. When it was only Sue and Jude, how they lived and what people said only mattered to them. But once Little Father Time becomes their responsibility and their own children are born, village gossip affects the littlest members of the family, too. Discuss whether their shame and disgrace is their fault or the fault of society.

2. Arabella says that she has taken up religion. Discuss the difference between people whose religious beliefs include kindness, generosity, charity, and forgiveness and people whose ideas of religion is limited to telling others what to do.

3. Describe the events in this section from the point of view of Little Father Time. Discuss his character.

4. Little Father Time is merely a child, but he has a major effect on the novel. He is living with Jude and Sue because Arabella would not accept the responsibility for caring for him. He was not christened to save the expense of a Christian burial. How might these things influence his behavior? Why do you think Hardy created this character and these circumstances?

"At Christminster Again"

New Characters:

Jack Stagg: *stonemason who recognizes Jude during the Remembrance Day celebration at Christminster*

Woman: *comments on Jude's fatigued appearance*

Coach Driver: *man who savagely mistreats his horse; Jude is shocked by the way he kicks his horse*

Policeman: *quiets crowd at Remembrance Day procession*

Landladies: *reject Jude's and Sue's requests for housing*

Third Landlady's Husband: *orders his wife not to house Sue and Jude*

Two Children: *offspring of Jude and Sue*

Surgeon: *tries to help the children*

Uncle Joe and Other Men: *guests at the second wedding of Jude and Arabella*

Summary

At the beginning of "At Christminster Again," Jude, Sue, and the children return to Christminster. There are crowds gathering for a Remembrance Day procession. Jude gets caught up in a conversation about Latin and architecture and is soon expounding to a throng his love for the university, his hopes of becoming a scholar, and the sad effect of poverty on him. The family then begins to look for lodging and is rejected in two places. The third takes them, but says that they may only stay a week once Sue confesses that she and Jude are not married. Jude then goes to stay at an inn.

One evening, in Chapter II, Little Father Time, who knows the family is having problems, becomes morbidly upset and says that children should be killed if they are a burden on their parents. Sue then tells him that she is expecting a third child. In the morning, she goes out to get Jude and when she comes back she finds that Little Father Time has hanged the others and himself. The surgeon arrives too late to save them. Sue blames herself and is inconsolable. Shortly thereafter, the baby is born dead.

In Chapter III, Sue becomes fanatically religious. She believes that she caused the death of the children by violating moral laws. She spends much of her time in the church she previously shunned. Jude still wants to get married, but Sue says that she feels that she is still married to Phillotson. Arabella comes over, as she has heard about the child. Her father is back from Australia and she is living with him. Sue then tells Jude that she felt there was justice in her children killing Sue's. She says that she loves Jude but that she must leave him. She goes off to live by herself.

In Chapter IV, Phillotson learns from Arabella the news of the children's deaths and the separation of Jude and Sue. Phillotson writes to Gillingham, asking his opinion on the possibility of Phillotson writing to Sue and asking her to return. Gillingham advises against

it, but Phillotson goes ahead, attempting to make the proposal sound sensible. Sue accepts the proposal. When she tells Jude, she is somewhat self-righteous, but gives him only praise.

Sue and Phillotson prepare to be married quickly in Chapter V. In order to punish herself, Sue turns away pretty clothes in favor of plain ones. Widow Edlin tells Phillotson that she believes that Sue does not really wish to marry him. Phillotson almost relents, but Gillingham urges him on and, in the end, the ceremony takes place.

Arabella comes to Jude in Chapter VI and asks to stay, saying that her father has thrown her out. Jude finds out through her that Sue has married. He and Arabella go out drinking in Marygreen, after which she takes him to her father's house; the story of being thrown out was a ruse to get Jude back.

Arabella tells yet another lie in Chapter VII when she tricks him into marriage, telling him that he had promised her while drunk. Tinker Taylor, Uncle Jim, and Uncle Joe, as well as some prostitutes, spend the night at Arabella's father's, drinking and playing cards. Early in the morning, Jude and Arabella go out and get married.

Jude becomes very sick and in Chapter VIII asks Arabella to send for Sue. She consents, provided that she can be in the room when Sue is there. Arabella does not send for Sue and finally Jude travels to Marygreen in inclement weather, even though he is weak and sick. He finds Sue at the school and they have an emotional meeting and kiss. This is their last encounter.

In Chapter IX, Jude returns to Christminster, where Arabella meets him at the station. On the way home he hears the same ghosts that he heard when he first came to live in the city. He tells Arabella he wanted to see Sue and to die, and that by traveling in the rain he might accomplish both.

In Marygreen, Sue tells Widow Edlin of her feelings for Jude. However, she says she must stay with Phillotson to punish herself. She then confesses to Phillotson that she kissed Jude and agrees to begin sleeping with Phillotson to atone. As with her refusal of attractive clothes, she is attempting to punish herself for the children's deaths.

In Chapter X, Jude, ill again, receives a visit from Widow Edlin, who discloses that Sue is with Phillotson to punish herself. Physician Vilbert also visits, but Jude sends him away. Arabella flirts with the doctor and allows him to kiss her.

Chapter XI, the final chapter in the novel, takes place on Remembrance Day. Jude is very ill, but Arabella goes out. Finally feeling remorseful, she returns home to find that Jude has died. She leaves him, goes out to rejoin the festivities and later makes arrangements to have him laid out. Widow Edlin comes to the funeral and tells Arabella that Sue is worn and sad. The novel ends with Arabella's statement that Sue will never be happy until she is dead now that Jude is gone.

Analysis

The novel ends with a melodramatic outpouring. First, Jude waxes sentimental at the Remembrance Day festivities. Little Father Time kills himself and the other children in a melancholy fit. Sue loses control, and becomes fanatical and masochistic. Despite the horror, there is a sense of catharsis. As in Greek drama, the tragedy destroys the malaise and has a purging effect. To take the analogy a step further, it can be said that the calamity is the result of tragic flaws within Jude and Sue. Jude's tragic flaw would be his kindness and idealism; Sue's would be idealism, but also willfulness.

Certainly, Sue's willfulness causes problems. All along she stands up to popular opinion, only to give in completely in previous sections. She compounds problems by being too forthright and impractical, as when she confesses to the landlady that she and Jude are not married. Her conversation with Little Father Time also seems foolish and insensitive. Rather than attempting to shield him from the concerns of the adult world, she compounds his worries with news of her pregnancy.

In thinking of *Jude* as a tragedy, however, it would be incorrect to see it entirely as a tragedy of character. Fate seems inextricably involved; the belief in a family curse contributes to this. It also seems that fate is a function of social forces. The power that keeps Jude and Sue apart is not entirely distinct from that which draws them together. At several times in "At Christminster" it seems that certain aspects of the disaster could be averted. In addition to the effects of Sue's thoughtless remark, the novel at other points seems on the verge of resolving in favor of Jude and Sue when someone or something pushes against them. Phillotson almost relents and cancels the wedding. Arabella almost sends for Sue. However, overall, the odds are clearly against a happy ending.

After the children's deaths, Jude and Sue contemplate the question of fate and essentially draw opposite conclusions. Jude accepts the tragedy as a random act of fate. Sue, however, personifies fate and sees it working to specifically punish her for her wrong-doing. She sees that the only way to overcome the horror is to atone through self-abnegation. "We must conform," she says to Jude.

In terms of the structure of the novel, the return to Christminster suggests that Jude and Sue have no more places to run. They are returning to the place where they first met. In a sense, the status quo has been preserved. The fruits of Jude and Sue's relationship are destroyed. Their children are dead, and Jude and Sue have returned to their original spouses. The warnings of Great-Aunt Drusilla seem justified, but again there is the sense that accepting the prediction of disaster is a self-fulfilling prophecy.

The opening chapter of this section contains many parallels to the story of the birth of Christ. Like Mary and Joseph, Sue and Jude are not married, and are refused a place to stay. Little Father Time is a perverse Christ-figure. He martyrs himself and his siblings to save his parents. However, his actions do not save anyone.

Earlier in the novel, Jude has frequently seen himself as emulating Christ. He wishes to begin his ministry at thirty, as Jesus did. Like Jesus, he is excluded from institutions of power. His speech to the crowd in the beginning of "At Christminster" is a sort of Sermon on the Mount. His death seems one of a martyr.

The tension between Old and New Testament philosophy, which has been evident throughout the novel, takes on a new twist. Sue begins to quote the New Testament, as Jude has done all along. However, while Jude had seen love, Sue's interpretation is one of pain and suffering. She quotes Corinthians. Hardy clearly evokes the story of Job in *Jude*. When Sue quotes Christian doctrine, Jude finds himself horrified that he had once believed so fervently. Jude, just before he dies, quotes a mournful verse from Job. Thus, he has reverted to the Old Testament.

"At Christminster" resounds with echoes of earlier parts of the novel. Each of Sue's weddings is followed by a death—the first by Aunt Drusilla's and the second by Jude's. Once again, Arabella tricks Jude into marriage as she did in "At Marygreen". Arabella finds a middle-aged suitor in Physician Vilbert, as Sue found one in Phillotson. Sue's feeling that she truly belongs to Phillotson mirrors Jude's initial belief that he was still Arabella's husband even after she left him. Even within "At Christminster", there is symmetry. The section both begins and ends on Remembrance Day. This reflexiveness creates a feeling of repetition and hopelessness; more optimistically, it may also create a sense of completion as the pattern may have worn itself out.

Malthus is a nineteenth-century theoretician whose influence can be seen in this section of *Jude*. Malthus predicted that the world's population would grow exponentially. He felt that starvation and epidemics were necessary to halt the population growth. Little Father Time's belief that the family's problems are the result of too many children echoes this theory.

Literary critics have often questioned the necessity of the suicide-murders, the most grotesque event in the novel. It destroys the sense of realism and takes the story to the level of allegory. The effect of the deaths is to destroy all external links between Jude and Sue. Little Father Time is something of an unknown factor, at this point resembling neither Arabella nor Jude.

There is a sense that because he was born in Australia, the product of a new country, he is extremely intense. The "father" in Little Father Time suggests that, paradoxically, the New World is more tied to the past than the Old. If Little Father Time is not a realistic figure, he seems instead to be a representation both biblical and of the excesses of imperialism. He knows evil, not necessarily because he has been ill-treated, but intrinsically. This episode is not the only way in which *Jude* departs from realism. Phillotson's willingness to allow Sue her freedom seems contrived. Also, the complete misfortune that befalls Jude seems almost as extreme and unlikely as the fortuitous coincidences of earlier Victorian novels.

The drunken locals tend to appear at low points in Jude's life—at the bar in Christminster after he is rejected and Phillotson falls for Sue, and again after Arabella has tricked him into marriage. They are much in evidence at the end of "At Christminster". In *Far from the Madding Crowd*, Hardy treats such groups of villagers more affectionately, but in *Jude*, they seem affiliated with Arabella. They bring out the worst in Jude.

In *Jude*, sex and death are clearly present, but there is very little sense of hope. Hardy seems to be extremely pessimistic. The eventual triumph of Arabella speaks ill of the values of the society about which Hardy wrote. Love does not succeed, but rather, social custom and pettiness. It could also be said that in the end, class boundaries prevail, as Sue goes back to her middle-class husband and Jude to his working-class wife. This would contradict the standard Victorian notion of progress and social improvement. Although *Jude* is sometimes considered a feminist novel, traditional marriage and male dominance win out. All that Sue would seem to have gained is wiped away with her return to Phillotson and her sexual submission to him. While not portraying this submission in a positive manner, Hardy is not holding out much hope for someone who defies male hierarchy. This was, of course, also true for *Tess of the D'Urbervilles*.

One of the major issues to pervade *Jude* is that of will and determinism. Literary critics seem to agree that the novel denies the existence of God, but acknowledges the working of a malevolent will. The forces of class, sexism, and hypocritical morality seem agents of this will. For Jude and Sue, there is no escape. It is not surprising, then, that after the completion of *Jude*, Hardy turned to writing poetry. The world that the novelist had created, or at least depicted, seemed too barren and hopeless to bear a successor.

Study Questions

1. Who is to be in the procession at Christminster?

2. What does Little Father Time say in the note he leaves behind?

3. Where do Sue and Phillotson get married?

4. What does Arabella tell Widow Edlin after the funeral that Jude did not want her to do?

5. Where do Arabella and Jude live when they are first remarried?

6. Where does Sue begin to go to church after the children's murders-suicide?

7. What confession does Sue make to her husband after Jude's visit?

8. What job does Sue have when she goes back to Phillotson?

9. What do Arabella and Widow Edlin hear in the distance as Jude is being buried?

10. Who are the only people standing by Jude's coffin?

Answers

1. The academic dons of the university are to be in the procession at Christminster.

2. The note says, "Done because we are too menny."

3. Sue and Phillotson are married in Marygreen.

4. Arabella tells Widow Edlin that Jude did not want to send for Sue.

5. Arabella and Jude live at her father's house.

6. She begins to attend St. Silas' Church.

7. Sue tells her husband that Jude visited and kisses were exchanged.

8. Sue begins teaching again.

9. They hear the conferring of honorary degrees.

10. Widow Edlin and Arabella are the only two people standing by Jude's coffin.

Suggested Essay Topics

1. Having finished the novel, what is your opinion of Sue? Did she do something wrong or is she simply the victim of social pressures? To what extent is Jude to blame? Use evidence from the whole novel to support your opinion.

2. Discuss the Biblical imagery in this section. Use examples from the text.

3. Hardy stated that he did not believe that in writing *Jude* he expressed an opinion on feminism or marriage. Do you think that an opinion emerges from the novel? Cite specific examples from the novel.

Sample Analytical Paper Topics

Topic #1

Discuss the hypothesis that the Bible is the philosophical and metaphoric underpinning of *Jude the Obscure*.

Outline

I.   Thesis Statement: *Religion plays a large role in the lives of the characters in* Jude the Obscure *and they frequently see events in biblical terms.*

II. Discussion of nineteenth-century views on the Bible and religion

   A. Jude's religious views

      1. Conflict between religion and scholarship

      2. Burning of religious books

      3. Personal religious feeling vs. morality

III. Religion in Sue's life

   A. Rebellion against tradition

   B. Conversion and fanaticism

IV. Views of other characters

   A. Arabella

   B. Phillotson

   C. Great Aunt Drusilla

V.   The Bible as a metaphor in *Jude*

    A.   Names in the novel

        1.   "At Marygreen"

        2.   "At Christminster"

Topic #2

Jude aspires to a university education. Discuss Jude's exclusion from the university.

Outline

I.   Thesis Statement: *The frustration Jude feels at being excluded from the university brings about his demise.*

II.   Jude's initial adulation of Phillotson

    A.   Learning of Greek and Latin

III.   Jude in Christminster

    A.   Link between desire for education and desire for Sue

    B.   Conflict between education and religion

    C.   Attitude of the authorities at Christminster

    D.   Sue's influence on Jude

    E.   Jude's encounter with the undergraduates

IV.   The destruction of Jude's dream

    A.   Burning of religious books

    B.   Attempts at marriage

    C.   Jude's speech at Christminster

Topic #3

Discuss the importance of churches and church architecture in *Jude the Obscure*.

Outline

I.   Thesis Statement: *Churches are focal points in* Jude the Obscure.

II. Hardy's architectural background

    A. Training

    B. Views

III. Jude's occupation

    A. Cathedral rebuilding in Christminster

    B. Painting the ten commandments in Albrickham

IV. Churches as settings within the plot

    A. Sue's opinions on churches

    B. Jude's escape to a church in Marygreen

    C. The wedding at Melchester

    D. Sue's retreat to St. Silas after the death of the children

Topic #4

Discuss the use of poetry in *Jude the Obscure*.

Outline

I. Thesis Statement: *Poetry, particularly that of Shelley, adds a significant dimension to the novel.*

II. The significance of poetry in the relationship between Jude and Sue

    A. Jude's sentimentality and love of beauty

    B. Sue's search for spiritual freedom

III. Shelley's poetry in *Jude the Obscure*

    A. "The Revolt of Islam"

    B. "Epipsychidion"

IV. Other poets in *Jude the Obscure*

    A. Milton

    B. Browning

    C. "Too Late"

    D. "The Worst of It"

    E. Quotes that open chapters

Topic #5

Discuss the influence of J. S. Mill and Edward Gibbon in *Jude the Obscure.*

Outline

I.   Thesis Statement: *Philosophy, particularly that of the English philosophers Mill and Gibbon, plays an important role, both implicitly and explicitly, in the novel.*

II.   Jude's philosophical readings

    A. Biblical

    B. Greek

III. Sue's philosophical reading

    A. Gibbon

    B. Mill

    C. "On Liberty"

    D. Mill's "On the Subjection of Women" as background to *Jude*

Topic #6

The women in *Jude the Obscure* are creations who show different sides to the female personality and identity.

Outline

I.   Thesis Statement: *The female characters in* Jude the Obscure *are diverse and represent different aspects of the female identity.*

II.   Characterizations of the women in the novel

    A. Jude's great-aunt is a staple of literature of the era, she is old-fashioned

        1. Jude's aunt compares him with Sue for being as crazy for books as Sue is

        2. She is conservative and cautions Jude to stay away from Sue

B. Arabella is drawn as a coarsely sensual schemer who entraps the naive and innocent Jude

    1. Arabella tricks Jude into marrying her. She claims she is pregnant

    2. Arabella wears a hairpiece and can produce dimples at will—proving she is false, this contrasts with Jude's innocence

C. Sue is presented as intellectual and pure

    1. Sue chooses not to consummate her marriage

    2. Sue does not consummate her relationship with Jude, even though they are so desperate to be together they wreck their lives

    3. Sue makes speeches about the lack of dignity in conventional marriages

III. Conclusion: The women in the novel are creations who show different sides to the female personality

SECTION FOUR

Bibliography

Abrams, M. H., et al., eds. *The Norton Anthology of English Literature, Vol. II.* New York: W. W. Norton, 1979.

Baker, Ernest A. *The History of the English Novel, Vol. 9.* New York: Barnes and Noble, 1936.

Bloom, Harold, ed. *Thomas Hardy's* Jude the Obscure. New York: Chelsea House Publishers, 1987.

Boumehla, Penny. *Thomas Hardy and Women: Sexual Ideology and Narrative Form.* Sussex: Harvester Press, 1982.

Carpenter, Richard. *Thomas Hardy.* Boston: Twayne Publishers, 1964.

Drabble, Margaret and Stringer, Jenny. *The Concise Oxford Companion to English Literature.* New York: Oxford University Press, 1990.

Hardy, Thomas. *The Collected Letters of Thomas Hardy,* Vol. 2: 1893–1901. R. L. Purdy and M. Millgate, eds. Oxford: Clarendon Press, 1980.

Hardy, Thomas. *Jude the Obscure.* New York: Penguin, 1978.

Howe, Irving. *Thomas Hardy.* New York: Macmillan, 1985.

Morgan, Rosemarie. *Women and Sexuality in the Novels of Thomas Hardy.* New York: Routledge, 1988.

Watts, Cedric. *Jude the Obscure.* New York: Penguin, 1992.

MAXnotes®

REA's Literature Study Guides

MAXnotes® are student-friendly. They offer a fresh look at masterpieces of literature, presented in a lively and interesting fashion. **MAXnotes®** offer the essentials of what you should know about the work, including outlines, explanations and discussions of the plot, character lists, analyses, and historical context. **MAXnotes®** are designed to help you think independently about literary works by raising various issues and thought-provoking ideas and questions. Written by literary experts who currently teach the subject, **MAXnotes®** enhance your understanding and enjoyment of the work.

Available **MAXnotes®** include the following:

Absalom, Absalom!
The Aeneid of Virgil
Animal Farm
Antony and Cleopatra
As I Lay Dying
As You Like It
The Autobiography of
    Malcolm X
The Awakening
Beloved
Beowulf
Billy Budd
The Bluest Eye, A Novel
Brave New World
The Canterbury Tales
The Catcher in the Rye
The Color Purple
The Crucible
Death in Venice
Death of a Salesman
The Divine Comedy I: Inferno
Dubliners
Emma
Euripedes' Electra & Medea
Frankenstein
Gone with the Wind
The Grapes of Wrath
Great Expectations
The Great Gatsby
Gulliver's Travels
Hamlet
Hard Times

Heart of Darkness
Henry IV, Part I
Henry V
The House on Mango Street
Huckleberry Finn
I Know Why the Caged
    Bird Sings
The Iliad
Invisible Man
Jane Eyre
Jazz
The Joy Luck Club
Jude the Obscure
Julius Caesar
King Lear
Les Misérables
Lord of the Flies
Macbeth
The Merchant of Venice
The Metamorphoses of Ovid
The Metamorphosis
Middlemarch
A Midsummer Night's Dream
Moby-Dick
Moll Flanders
Mrs. Dalloway
Much Ado About Nothing
My Antonia
Native Son
1984
The Odyssey
Oedipus Trilogy

Of Mice and Men
On the Road
Othello
Paradise Lost
A Passage to India
Plato's Republic
Portrait of a Lady
A Portrait of the Artist
    as a Young Man
Pride and Prejudice
A Raisin in the Sun
Richard II
Romeo and Juliet
The Scarlet Letter
Sir Gawain and the
    Green Knight
Slaughterhouse-Five
Song of Solomon
The Sound and the Fury
The Stranger
The Sun Also Rises
A Tale of Two Cities
Taming of the Shrew
The Tempest
Tess of the D'Urbervilles
Their Eyes Were Watching God
To Kill a Mockingbird
To the Lighthouse
Twelfth Night
Uncle Tom's Cabin
Waiting for Godot
Wuthering Heights

RESEARCH & EDUCATION ASSOCIATION
61 Ethel Road W. • Piscataway, New Jersey 08854
Phone: (908) 819-8880

Please send me more information about MAXnotes®.

Name _____

Address _____

City _____ State _____ Zip _____

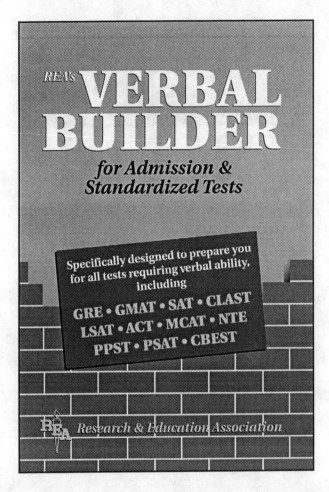

Available at your local bookstore or order directly from us by sending in coupon below.

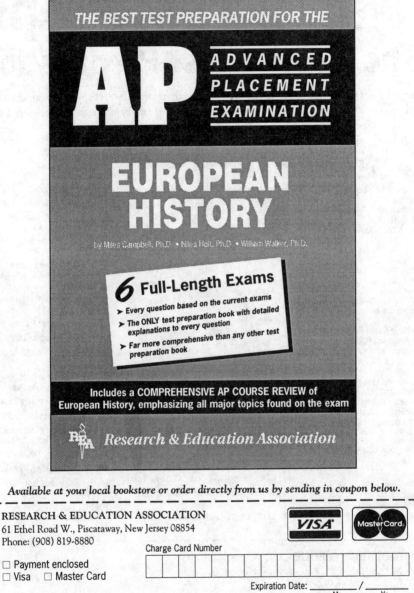